KILLING
COMPLACENCY

Resurrect Ambition.
Maximize Your Life.

PAUL J HUBER

Killing Complacency
Resurrect Ambition. Maximize Your Life.

Disclaimer
This book contains the ideas and opinions of its author. It is designed to provide entertainment to readers. The intention of this book is to provide information, helpful content and motivation to readers about on the subjects addressed. It is shared and sold with the understanding that the author is not engaged to render any type of opinions, psychological, medical, legal or any other kind of personal or professional advice. The author has tried to recreate events, locales and conversations from memories of them. In order to maintain their anonymity in some instances, names of individuals and places may have been changed. Identifying characteristics and details such a physical properties, occupations and places of residence may have been changed as well. No warranties or guarantees are expressed or implied by the author's choice to include any of the content in this volume. The author shall not be liable for any physical, psychological, emotional, financial or commercial damages, including, but not limited to, special, incidental, consequential or other damages. The reader is responsible for their own choices, actions and results.

Scripture quotations marked MSG are taken from THE MESSAGE, copyright © 1993, 2002, 2018 by Eugene H. Peterson. Used by permission of NavPress. All rights reserved. Represented by Tyndale House Publishers, a Division of Tyndale House Ministries. Scripture quotations marked (NIV) are taken from the Holy Bible, New International Version®, (NIV)®. Copyright © 1973, 1978, 1984, 2011 by Biblica, Inc.™ Used by permission of Zondervan.

KILLING

1st edition, 1st printing 2020
Cover design by: Steve Walters at Oxygen Publishing (www.oxygenpublishing.com)
Interior design by: Steve Walters
Author photo by Jacob Huber

ISBN: 9798648455979
Imprint: Independently published

Feel free to share pop-out quotes and your Killing Complacency reading experience on social media.

Use #killingcomplacency, and tag me to spread the word of this book. More people need the hope that it provides.

—Paul Huber

WHY I WROTE THIS BOOK

AND WHY YOU NEED TO READ IT

I wrote this book because I have felt the oppression of complacency in my own life. What follows is the reconciliation of contentment without complacency; healthy ambition without envy; and a guide for setting the trajectory to your destiny.

If you want to overcome the modern scourge of complacency, then read on.

> *The world is full of people in need, but perhaps the greatest need is for an end to complacency and limiting beliefs.*
> **—Paul Huber**

KILLING

KILLING COMPLACENCY

TABLE OF CONTENTS

KILLING

COMPLACENCY

Before proceeding, download your bonus content at **pauljhuber.com/ kc-bonuses**

KILLING

CHAPTER ONE

UNLIMITED LONGINGS

I know you have felt it. I have. We all have. It's the desire for more than you already have. More money; more belongings; more time; more sex; more food; more, more, more. The desire is insatiable, unending, and universal. Like any other human instinct, the results may be constructive or destructive. From useful goods, services, and the propagation of the species to deception, adultery, and war, the urge brings a wide range of results. Marketers leverage our urges for more, in ways that drive sales—which can be good for them but bad for our debt levels.

The urge for more is as natural as a lion hunting its prey—it's a normal instinct that should not surprise any of us. Instead, we need to know how to respond effectively.

THE URGE FOR MORE

Society, through education, culture, and religion, has sought to minimize the destructive side of our unlimited longings, but in many ways has overcorrected—leading to complacency. For every person who avoids destructively pursuing more, another avoids constructively pursuing more. For every person who follows scripture to abundance, there are a thousand more who use it, and misquote it, to build complacency. Modern America's propensity to use scripture to discourage pursuing success is one of the reasons there is so much of it in the following pages. Believers should see that God is more like a tough physical trainer than a genie. If you think God, the universe, or fate, just wants to drop you into your destiny, you will never achieve what you are really designed to do.

The push of society to complacency is not the only contributor though. The nature of any animal is to conserve energy as much as possible. The big cats of the African savannah rarely exhibit their notable speed—instead they lounge most of the day, and only occasionally sprint as they attempt to kill their next meal. It's our conflicting nature to both want more, and conserve energy in ways which prevent us from having more.

> *The urge for more is not wrong or unholy—it's only our response to it that **may** be.*
> —**Paul Huber** *Killing Complacency*

Properly focusing and directing our urge for more allows us to overcome our nature of conserving energy.

KILLING

Mitigating the negative side of wanting more allows us to overcome the complacency embedded within our minds.

Feeling stuck in or bored by a job does not mean taking it was the wrong thing—instead, the feeling is like hunger; though you were previously satisfied, it's now time for more. Is it time to do what it takes to push into the next thing? Dana White, who grew the UFC from being worth a few million to being worth a few billion, says that if it kills you to go to work, then it's time to take the next step to a different job.

Not to say you should quit in dramatic fashion like you saw in a movie—instead, take prudent steps to prepare for the next move.

THE QUEST FOR MEANING

In addition to our animal drive for food, safety, and procreation and our human drive for accumulating and experiencing more, humans have a deep drive for meaning. Leaders and managers seeking to motivate their team members often overlook the power of giving meaning to the work—beyond having a paycheck that provides for personal and family needs. The reason any job exists is the expectation of it being integral to producing something a customer is willing to buy.

It's easy to feel disconnected from the meaning a job should provide, when leadership does not help articulate how that job, or the company, contributes to meeting the needs of customers and society.

Employees disconnect further because of jobs filled with unneeded or wasteful activity. Underlying movements like Lean Manufacturing (the Toyota Production System) and Six Sigma is the realization that the modern workplace includes activities for which customers do not want to pay, and defects that could be avoided. How much more meaningful could work be if it focused on creating greater value!

The meaning, though, is not in the work itself but the outcomes it produces. The meaning is not in a specific job or form of success; the meaning is in having a job that contributes to a business, your survival, and driving toward continuing or future success. In fact, the best way to derive meaning from a job is to continually push for improvement, so the organization can serve the most people with the least effort and cost.

We are barraged with people telling us to find meaning by feeding the hungry, saving the whales, and praying for world peace. None of which are bad, but all are overwhelming to the average individual. It's better to start by finding meaning where you are; then finding ways to contribute to a few causes that are most important to you.

Instead of feeling pressured to change the whole world, seek to maximize your impact in the part of the world where you spend the most time—your work. Seek to maximize your impact on those closest to you—your friends, family, and the local community.

Combining the healthy aspects of the urge for more with your natural quest for meaning causes unhealthy

and destructive behaviors to fall away, because there is no time or energy left for anything detracting from your goal.

SUCCESS IS YOUR DUTY

> *Success is my duty, obligation, and responsibility.*
> —Grant Cardone

Some of the earliest inspirations for this book were the result of spending three days at Grant Cardone's second 10X Growth Conference. Grant, similar to the late Zig Ziglar before him, is a sales training and motivational guru (it's funny how those two often go together). Rather than selling just books and tapes, Grant uses twenty-first-century technology to deliver online training to sales professionals. Through his books and social media, Grant also provides healthy levels of motivation and inspiration to millions of Americans. As Zig said, "People often say that motivation doesn't last. Well, neither does bathing—that's why we recommend it daily."

Part of my daily motivation is understanding that because I have been given much, much is expected of me. Not because Grant or any human says success is my duty, but because of some the parables Jesus told.

Take a look at the Parable of the Talents (Matt 25:14-30) or the Parable of the Minas (Luke 19:12-27). In both situations, a master puts his servants in charge of some of his wealth when he goes away for a long while. Based on his prior experience with his employees, the master knows to trust some more than others. When the master returns, he sees his trust in the best two validated—each then receives more responsibility. However, the one entrusted with little proves he is unworthy of trust. The result is the little he has is taken from him (and in Luke's account, he is killed in front of the master).

In the modern era, when Jack Welch was CEO of GE, he ensured the best (top 20%) were treated very well—similar to the servant who grew 5 talents to 10, they were given what was taken from the worst performers. The middle 70% were still treated well—like the servant given 2 talents and grew it to 4. And the bottom 10% knew they needed to find a new job… but nobody was ever killed or cast into "outer darkness." (Welch, 2009)

Whenever I read a parable, I have to remind myself it's not an account of an actual event from which we should learn. Instead, it's a carefully crafted allegory where Jesus chose the plot and the ending. Why is the man of little ability not forgiven for his failings, stripped of his little bit of money, treated harshly, and even killed? What is this business of the low performer sniveling about the master reaping where he did not sow? To me, the master (God) has already given the servant (me) all of the resources (capacity, ability, and

opportunity) required for a bountiful harvest. If I do not return the level of results expected, the resources invested in me are wasted.

Certainly, God desires I seek him out, I listen to His still, small voice, and I learn how His power manifests as my faith in Him grows. However, I am also expected to make the most of what has been entrusted to me.

In fact, in 1 Corinthians 3:10-15, we see the believer who does not accomplish their calling with the right motives will avoid eternity in hell, but will not receive a greater eternal reward for a life well-lived. Because passion, purpose, and calling are such important topics, Chapter 10 explores the truth of each—and it's not what you expected.

In all areas, body, being, balance, and business, success is my duty, my obligation, and my respon-sibility. (White, 2017) I cannot be "reasonable" in accepting less than what I was created for. (Cardone, 2011) I cannot be complacent in accepting the status quo. I must be content to press on toward the goal.

The expectation of success is not for any single event to succeed or for you to continually be at the top. Instead, the expectation of success should lead to the continual pursuit of improvement and advancement—even if it comes with setbacks and failures along the way. Failure is an event—not a permanent status or title.

Perhaps you feel like little is expected of you because you have been given little. However, know that it takes zero natural talent to show up on time and be polite—yet that is better than what many people manage to muster. Ultimately, natural ability makes a smaller contribution than attitude and consistent behavior.

If you are going to spend countless hours—thousands of them—supporting your survival, why not make the most of them? If you are giving your time, the substance of your life to something, why not make the most of it? Growing in skill and responsibility, rather than just passing the time.

KILLING THE FIXED MINDSET

Killing the hydra of complacency begins with killing the fixed mindset. Whether you feel you were given one or five talents, your responsibility is to do the most you can with what you have. Maximizing what you have starts with believing the required growth is within your reach.

> *Every master was once a disaster.*
> *—T. Harv Eker*

The path to abundance begins with believing growth is possible. Unfortunately, much of society—down to our parents and teachers during our formative years—reinforces the fixed mindset. It's completely

contradictory but true, the same people who feed us the message that we can be anything, more frequently reinforce the fixed mindset.

Society leads us to dream about glamorous or prestigious jobs like professional athlete, celebrity, or president, and then we are told not to outshine our peers too much. "Don't look too good—you make them look bad." In some parts of our culture, the psychological and social equivalent of the old caste system is built through peer pressure, to limit the desire and acceptability of growth. (Sowell, 2005)

In her book *Mindset: The New Psychology of Success*, psychologist Carol Dweck, Ph. D. defines two mindsets: "fixed" and "growth." Those with the fixed mindset believe their intellectual and physical abilities are as immutable as their shoe size or stature. With a fixed mindset, one only pursues the areas where they show a "natural aptitude."

With a growth mindset, you can first be realistic about where you are, and then choose the areas to grow in and pursue. Having a growth mindset correlates directly to successful results as Dweck demonstrated in empirical studies. (Dweck, 2006)

Digging deeper into the growth mindset, in *Talent is Overrated: What Really Separates World-Class Performers from Everybody Else,* we see results are less about any type of innate ability, and more about executing the deliberate practice needed to get better. (Colvin, 2008) Certainly, each person has different levels of physical and intellectual capacity—the realism side of the growth mindset. However, the differentiator, the thing actually setting one person apart from the next, is the amount of deliberate practice. (Erickson & Pool, 2006)

The reality for the NBA star is being tall—taller than 99% of the population—is generally required to get into the top echelons of the game. The reality for the professional horse racing jockey is being in the bottom few percentiles of height and weight, is the only way to provide the best opportunity for the horse to win. However, this size-based reality is only the essential entry criteria; to achieve world-class results, countless hours of learning, drilling, and preparing are required. And only those who augment their current position with the best coaching accomplish the next level of success.

The importance of the right mindset is not a new concept. In 1937, Napoleon Hill explored it in *Think and Grow Rich*. Inspired by a suggestion from railroad magnate Andrew Carnegie, Hill studied numerous successful people for years. His conclusions recognized that success starts in the mind, and through diligent action with definiteness of purpose success works its way into the physical world. (Hill, 1937)

My son, Jacob, learned to juggle by watching YouTube videos and by practicing—a lot. He has progressed significantly in his skills, and now watching him juggle flaming torches is a special treat. During his journey to this level of expertise, he often repeated the Harv Eker

quote at the beginning of this section. Over and over, he dropped balls, juggling pins, and unlit torches as he prepared to juggle lit torches. His growth mindset and ability to build upon all of the other coordination skills he has, means he frequently adds new tricks to his skillset—after yet more deliberate practice.

For many of us, the fixed mindset has been embedded from a young age. A child with an insatiable appetite for candy at the checkout may be told by her budget-conscious parents "we can't afford it." Or a teen, wanting the latest fashion is told to buy the budget jeans. The reality is, most parents could afford the candy or the jeans, but they don't want to give out sugary treats and have other budgeting priorities.

The alternative approach, advocated by Robert Kiyosaki, is to evaluate what it would take to afford the desired object and not to make cost an excuse for not buying it. Quite reasonably though, he also encourages prioritizing spending on assets that make money rather than accumulating objects and expenses. (Kiyosaki, 2009)

SPECIAL BONUS OFFER
GO TO
pauljhuber.com/kc-bonuses
to download exclusive
content for readers of
Killing Complacency.

CHAPTER TWO

CONTENTMENT'S BIG LIE

> *Embedded in the wisdom of contentment is the big lie of complacency. Adjacent to avoiding ill-advised action is the inaction of complacency. The prudence of seeking wise counsel degrades easily into paralysis by analysis.*
>
> —**Paul Huber** *Killing Complacency*

Every remedy for the destructive behaviors associated with our unlimited longings presents a dichotomy between its proper application and the improper elimination of constructive action.

Surgically removing the lie of complacency from the wisdom of contentment leads to contentment without complacency and ambition without destructive selfishness.

THE THREAT OF COMPLACENCY

The greatest threat to the betterment of humanity is not an overtly evil dictator; it's not the poverty facing too many people; or the political divide America faces. Instead, the thing that is limiting our continued improvement is the cancer of complacency.

Complacency can creep up in all areas of our lives—body, being, balance, and business. Whether it's our health, our spiritual life, our significant relationships, or our earning ability, we need to be content without being complacent.

The need for discernment echoes through the following pages. The first challenge for discernment is the need to identify the difference between contentment and complacency—the former a lack of envy, the latter a lack of healthy ambition.

THE SCOURGE OF COMPLACENCY

Because of complacency, the average American is overweight (or obese), out of touch with their creator (or any belief in a higher power), miserable in their relationships, and broke. Body, being, balance, and business are all suffering.

I am not saying you should be ripped; believe in my God, married, and rich. I am saying that because of complacency, we are not achieving what we should, and all areas of our lives are suffering. As we kill complacency, you will see there are many roots to complacency, and the fruit is a diminished level of success in the world.

While trying and failing should produce learning that later leads to success, complacency is failing

before trying. Trying and failing may destroy some value on the road to success—the road to a net creation of value. On the other hand, failing through complacency decreases the amount of value a person provides to the world.

Whether you believe your calling echoed down from heaven or whispered through your interests (which we will explore more later), the scourge of complacency keeps too many from living the full life to which they were called.

CONTENTMENT VS. COMPLACENCY

It's hard to master contentment without complacency. Discerning the difference between taking a much-needed break to recharge and neglecting responsibility can be hard to spot. However, after showing how to differentiate between contentment and complacency, we will meet someone who mastered contentment without complacency.

Through cold and icy midwestern winters, I have learned the safe practice of contentment with the available traction—rather than spinning my wheels in a battle I'm sure to lose. Excessive attempts to accelerate on an icy road simply make ice worse. However, a measured and deliberate acceleration allows me to quickly reach the maximum reasonable speed for the road conditions. Contentment and realism about current conditions opens the door to changing the situation, whereas denial and flailing prevent actual progress.

COMPLACENCY

CONTENTMENT

My mental picture of contentment has often been a person who has accepted their lot in life, and learned to enjoy life despite their meager means. Perhaps feeding my image is, through years of attending church, I have often heard exhortations of contentment from Philippians 4: 12:

> *I know what it's to be in need, and I know what it's to have plenty. I have learned the secret of being content in any and every situation, whether well fed or hungry, whether living in plenty or in want. (NIV)*

Recently, though, I have noticed Paul learned contentment in *plenty* and in want—how can this be? I had been led to believe poverty was next to holiness. The secret is not how much one has, but their attitude to what they have and what others have—a concept explored more fully as we beat complacency to death.

The secret of contentment is a lack of envy and coveting:

- The content person maximizes what they have rather than longing for what they lack.
- Living below their current income, the content person is investing in themselves, their family, and their church, while also finding ways to grow their value and, as a result, their income.

 KILLING

- Being content means wisely discerning between get rich quick schemes enriching only the promoters, and wise strategies for growing wealth—which can also be expensive to learn.
- The content person asks, "what can I do with what I have?" rather than lamenting—if they only had something more, they could do more.
- Being content with your body means instead of feeling the shame about its current state, you recognize proper care is essential for your long-term happiness and wellbeing.

Those who are content in plenty avoid the sting of falling from their elevated station. They have learned that pursuing more is not about out-doing their competitors; instead, it's about being able to serve even more people through their work or business with a relentless pursuit of their purpose.

Contentment is more than just something yielding dividends in one's own life. Thomas Sowell describes multi-generational contentment in action, as immigrants from certain cultures living below their means to build businesses, and sending their children to college for valuable degrees—ones that pay back many times the cost of their investment. These immigrants understood contentment was for more than just the betterment of their own lives—it was to pay dividends for their children and grandchildren who would live much better than them. (Sowell, 2016)

The immigrant to America who is content but not complacent understands the opportunities available to themselves and their descendants. Many life-long American's instead see the country's shortcomings rather than its opportunities.

COMPLACENCY

While the content make-do with what they have, the complacent lack the drive to attain more. The content are realistic about their situation, while the complacent wallow in their situation. To differentiate the positive contentment from the negative complacency, ask yourself if you can do better, and what are you doing to make each of the areas of your life better—body, being, balance, and business.

Certainly, misapplied ambition and drive can be detrimental as we often see attempted shortcuts leading to disaster. However, the consequences of complacency are just as dire. Instead of flaming-out in spectacular fashion, the complacent just fade into the background—often with an air of holy contentment.

We are not on the earth merely to exist, complacent in our situation. Instead, we are here to produce abundant fruit in accordance with our God-given capacity to do so.

A content, mature fig tree ought to produce figs, given sufficient water and nutrients. One day, the creator of the universe was walking past such a tree, but it had no fruit at a time when it should have. Jesus cursed the tree, and it withered and died by the end of the day. (Mark 11:12-25)

 KILLING

The tree is like a person who thought they were being to content to survive where they were planted, but not realizing the opportunity they had to produce fruit. By failing to produce fruit, the tree was failing at its mission in life. Like so many people, the tree was dead; it just had not figured it out yet. If you are not producing the fruit for which you were created, you are as cursed as that fig tree... which is why I was afraid to *not* write this book.

It's important to remember there are seasons in which fruit is expected—and a certain fruit for you may not yet be in season. While the passage suggests it was too early to see ripe fruits, scholars suggest it was at a time when the tree should have had its first fruits—the ones required for offerings.

GRATITUDE

Maybe you have had an experience analogous to this: while visiting your grandmother, she gives you a piece of butterscotch candy from the bottom of her purse, when what you really wanted was one of her scrumptious apple dumplings. Being an impetuous child rather than a reserved adult, you complained that there were no apple dumplings available during your visit—and your mom scolded you for not being content with the gift.

The problem was not a lack of contentment, but a lack of gratitude. Someone generously offered you something that you didn't earn or have to buy.

Expressing gratitude for the life we have, the gifts that others offer us, and the opportunities within our situation is absolutely the right thing to do.

Taking the responsibility to learn how to make (or buy) your favorite dessert is the path to contentment without complacency. You can be grateful when you receive a gift *and* ambitious to earn what you desire. A cunning child would ask to learn in order to solve both the short-term and long-term desires for deliciousness.

Without gratitude, the path to contentment without complacency won't work. Without gratitude, the people with whom you work will not be motivated to help you. Without gratitude, God, the universe, or whatever you believe in, will not see fit to provide you with the next larger installment of blessing.

> *Gratitude provides the foundation for moving to the next goal or receiving the next blessing.*
>
> —**Paul Huber** *Killing Complacency*

CONTENTMENT WITHOUT COMPLACENCY

Contentment without complacency drives wise, ethical behaviors to achieve greater success. It drove

KILLING

the Apostle Paul to spread the Gospel across incredible distances. Philippians 3:10-14:

> *I want to know Christ—yes, to know the power of his resurrection and participation in his sufferings, becoming like him in his death, and so, somehow, attaining to the resurrection from the dead.*
>
> *Not that I have already obtained all this, or have already arrived at my goal, but **I press on** to take hold of that for which Christ Jesus took hold of me. Brothers and sisters, I do not consider myself yet to have taken hold of it. But one thing I do: Forgetting what is behind and **straining toward what is ahead**, **I press on toward the goal** to win the prize for which God has called me heavenward in Christ Jesus. [Emphasis mine]   (NIV)*

Paul learned to differentiate between contentment and complacency properly—he understood he must press on to live out his calling as an apostle, while also being content in his daily situation. Few are called to be apostles, yet *all* of us are called to press on to our particular calling.

COMPLACENCY   21

Paul understood his purpose in this world – he had what Napoleon Hill called a "definiteness of purpose." (Hill, 2012) By knowing what he was called to do with his limited time on earth, all of the things not leading to fulfillment of his purpose lost all appeal to him. The drive to his goal was far stronger than the allure of sinful behavior—even to the point where permissible, but not beneficial behavior was unappealing.

Contentment without complacency means you are willing to do the work required to achieve your calling. It means you understand there are no shortcuts to anywhere worth going, and discerning wise counsel from hype can help you safely accelerate the path to success.

The complacent accept the status quo, and fail to change themselves or their circumstances. Those who overcome complacency realize that if you do what you have always done, you are going to get what you always got… if your actions don't change, your results won't change. If nothing changes, then nothing changes.

Seeking safety is good when it aids in our discernment of the most prudent course—but too much safety brings death to our mission. I love the first line of the "Lion Chaser's Manifesto:" (Batterson, 2016)

> *Quit living as if the purpose of life is*
> *to arrive safely at death.*
>   —*Mark Batterson*

> *The complacent avoid risks, resulting in a meager existence. The overly ambitious rush headlong into risky situations. The discerning understands which risks are reasonable and which are excessive.*
> —**Paul Huber** *Killing Complacency*

MOURNING COMPLACENCY

Creating a new reality in our lives often means the death of an old reality—and death is often hard to accept. While it seems reasonable to mourn the passing of our loved ones, it may seem silly that we need to mourn the passing of the status quo. For example, when I found the need to reduce calorie and carb intake, I needed to mourn the end of my dessert filled life and celebrate the new eating lifestyle.

Near the start of my career, I was involved in a significant change initiative at work. The objective was not to change one thing but to change everything—to be "Lean" in the same way Toyota minimizes waste and maximizes profitability. One of my fellow change leaders explained to me that the process of change often resembles the mourning process for those whose world is being up-ended in the name of Lean, and they need to go through the same five stages of mourning just as someone who has lost a loved one – denial, anger, bargaining, depression, and (eventually) acceptance. (Kübler-Ross, 1973)

Of course, not all changes are mourned—from changing our clothes to upgrading our cell phones every two years or so, we relentlessly change much of our world. The model for *The Diffusion of Innovations* depicts some "early adopters" changing early, and a few "laggards" holding out until the old technology is no longer available—with the mass of the population in the middle. (Rogers, 2003)

The difference between mourning and celebrating change is the mindset of those who are coping with or pursuing the change. I hope you recognize complacency; see it for the threat it is, and desire to kill it everywhere you find it.

MOURNING THE WAY IT WAS

Though it is hard to miss what was holding you back, it's more likely that you will miss some of the things that you used to do. I don't miss being complacent, but I do miss some of the television shows that I used to watch. I don't miss it, but you may miss daylong marathons of watching sportsball.

Killing complacency is not the end of all leisure activity, but creating greater ambition will lessen the pull of other activities. Days of leisure will turn into days of active recovery and pursuit of accomplishing greater objectives.

As this book receives its final edits before publishing, we are several months into the COVID-19 pandemic. While much of the world is in denial about the permanent changes that will happen as a result, others have either moved through the mourning process, or are acting as if they had—accepting the changes.

Reaching acceptance of the new realities (or the fluidity of the situation) allows the proactive to seek the new opportunities provided within the pandemic. Physical distancing and quarantining required as part of the response, increases the opportunity for those who provide virtual social connections, delivery services, and condoms.

Instead of waiting for normal to return, which it may not, seek to thrive during and after the change. Use the opportunity—not as an opportunist to harm others, but to help others and to prepare yourself for the next phase.

COMPLACENCY

SPECIAL BONUS OFFER
GO TO
pauljhuber.com/kc-bonuses
to download exclusive
content for readers of
Killing Complacency.

CHAPTER THREE

RESCUING AMBITION

As we kill complacency, we need to resurrect ambition in its place. Where the weeds of complacency grew, we now need to plant and encourage healthy ambition. Having "definiteness of purpose," as Napoleon Hill put it, means a person will focus their energy on the objective rather than the transient pleasures distracting from it. (Hill, 2012)

Ambition driven by our desire to fulfill our purpose in life properly is critical to staying on the right path. Ambition driven solely by our unlimited longing for more is the path to destruction. In the afterword to *Rescuing Ambition*, Dave Harvey compares ambition to sex. "It's supposed to be an expression of who we are as human beings, but in many people's experience, it turns into, well, guilty frustration. Ambition seems to have an important function, but it gets complicated in real life. Just like sex." (Harvey, 2010)

RESURRECTING AMBITION

If our ambition derails into lying, cheating, and stealing to get ahead, we have gone down the wrong path. If instead, our ambition leads to hard work, focused effort to improve and add more value to those around us, and to serve the world through being the best version   of ourselves, then ambition has led to a better world and to fulfilling our calling.

> *Ambition is neither good nor bad; holy nor unholy. Our motives and actions surrounding our ambition* **are** *good or bad, holy or unholy.*
> —**Paul Huber** *Killing Complacency*

Ambition has gotten a bad name. Both from those who envy the success of others, and from the ambitious applying the wrong methods to achieving their success.

Rescuing ambition in our own lives means we need to focus our ambition on finding ways to help others while also providing profit for ourselves.

Rescuing our ambition in the world requires we suspend judgment on the ambition of others. Instead, as we interact with the ambitious, we need to be discerning about whether or not their request of us is in our best interest or not. Discerning our end of a bargain is far easier than judging the heart, which should be left up to the Omniscient One.

Perhaps the best analogy for our innate ambition is our drive for food. Both are necessary and life sustaining, and both can be hard to manage. With food, it's often easy to see the results of a poorly managed drive to eat, when someone is noticeably overweight or malnourished. A poorly managed ambition is often transparent to the world—only visible at the extremes of poverty or opulence.

THE WORLD NEEDS SUCCESS

Where would the world be without Henry Ford, Nicola Tesla, Bill Gates, Steve Jobs, and the men and women who surrounded them? Only those who could afford handcrafted, expensive cars would be driving; many of us would be in the dark due to the inefficiency of Edison's electric system; computers would be rare; smartphones would be just for executives. Or perhaps, all of these building blocks of our modern world would be delayed by years or decades.

Through the success of extraordinary men and women, we have experienced ever-growing levels of productivity and efficiency. Through the growth of productivity, we are able to produce goods and services far more efficiently than in years past—and to have things nobody imagined a century before. Even the richest person two centuries ago would not have had the ability to send a message as quickly as today, when just about anybody on earth can send a text message across the world nearly instantaneously. Their ability to see the world—in person or through the media—was nothing like we have today.

Even without the category-defining successes listed above, the availability and affordability of modern conveniences is astonishing. A recent comparison of products from 1979 to 2015 showed comparable goods dropping in price (including total dollars, inflation-adjusted dollars, and labor hours required to purchase). Continuous decreases in cost and increases in quality have allowed more people to afford more conveniences than ever before—even if the inflation-adjusted wages have not changed very much.

While affording more stuff is not the end-all in life, the ability to acquire more goods for less effort means we are able (in theory) to redirect our energies to other areas. The successful increase in productivity and trade means a smaller percentage of the population is in abject poverty than ever before.

THE WORLD NEEDS YOUR SUCCESS

It's not just the big successes and productivity improvements the world needs, though. The world needs more individuals—including you—to be successful. If we can kill complacency in many, we can move the average level of success. Moving the average level of success means helping more people in the process—either as they receive goods and services, or as they are employed in the process.

> *Success produces sustainable benefits in ways charity cannot. Charity is important, but it relies on the overflow of success. The process of successful commerce benefits all who are involved in producing it, resulting in the ability to produce even more.*
>
> —**Paul Huber** *Killing Complacency*

Your success is entirely about you AND entirely about the world around you. Having success without providing value ranges from empty to criminal. Providing value to the world around you is the only way to reap the success for which you were created. Being well equipped and continuously improving our ability to provide value in this ever-changing world, is key to staying relevant and well compensated.

Progress comes not just from revolutionary new ideas but also from the daily, incremental gains in quality, productivity, and individuals' own human capital. While it may seem like only select people are revolutionaries, we can all take part in daily, incremental improvements—to do as Jack Welch said, "find a better way every day." (Welch, 2009)

Whether you are leading a business or you are one of its front-line employees, maintaining healthy margins—profitability—is one of the most important parts of the job, through actions big and occasional or small and repetitive. Profitability means the business is providing value exceeding the cost of production. Profitability means the business is sustainable. Profitability means the business has an opportunity to grow, serving more customers, and employing more in the process.

Taking a loss—failing to be profitable—is not approaching holiness or some enlightened plane; instead, it's unsustainable, unwise, and poor stewardship. Indeed, not every business venture succeeds—sometimes life lessons are very expensive. However, making business decisions based on the likelihood of success and profit ensures a return on the effort, and that all involved are able to receive value through the process. (Whelchel, 2012)

Holiness comes in our handling of the profits—how much is reinvested, used for living, or given to help others. Once you have been a good steward in your business dealings, out of your take-home profit, consider prioritizing giving first, then saving, and spending last. This order will keep your budget from expanding to the income available, rather than being the result of strategic planning.

Real enlightenment in business creates value at every level: the production of value for customers which is greater than the price they pay, which is greater than the cost to produce, which includes compensating employees and suppliers fairly. Any time we fail to produce value in this way, we fail someone in the value chain.

THE FUTURE OF SUCCESS

Though many people fear the ever-increasing level of automation and artificial intelligence, these new frontiers of productivity improvements mean we can buy even more for less money. Increased automation will continue the decline in the number of people needed for manual labor. Instead, more people will need to do what only humans can do – providing a personal touch. Personality and attitude will be increasingly important factors in hiring decisions, the way they are for companies like Starbucks and Virgin. (Branson, 2014)

For those who are on the front lines of personal interaction rather than designing the automation, the best thing anybody can do to meet the increasing competition for providing exceptional service, is to improve their emotional intelligence. Emotional intelligence is not a fixed capacity, as many view intellectual capacity; instead, it's something that can be developed and honed to respond better to the people around you. (Bradberry, 2009)

Transitioning through the Industrial Revolution was undoubtedly painful for many as craftsmanship gave way to mass production. Transitioning further into the Automation Revolution will undoubtedly have its pains too. The best pain relief remedy is to use your human adaptability to find the success of the future—even if the exact form of your success is unexpected.

GROWING RICH IS THE AMERICAN DREAM—STAYING POOR IS GREEDY

Eliminating the old-world caste system that enforced the permanent separation of the nobility and the serfs, allows Americans and many in the west, to rise from destitute to loaded. In one longitudinal study of specific individuals, the University of Michigan found 95% of those who started in the bottom 20% of wage earners in 1975 were no longer there in 1991. Though an unfortunate 5% stayed at the bottom, 29% moved all the way to the top 20% of earners. (Cox & Alm, 1995)

Achieving the American dream in this way should be recognized and celebrated as people build the value of their skills in order to move up the economic ladder. In the same way a child moves from milk to strained foods to solids, to making their own foods, they should be expected to move from needing their parents' support, to taking care of themselves, to building their own empire and caring for their own offspring.

Allowing ourselves to be complacent not only robs us of the feeling of accomplishment, but it also deprives the rest of the world of the contributions we could have made—whether it's as beautiful as a work of art or as utilitarian as a well-mowed lawn.

The world has many who are in poverty, and as "Shark Tank" star Daymond John says, poverty of the bank account is temporary, but poverty of the mind is permanent. Meaning, it's possible to do as he did—moving out of poverty—but only if the mind is willing to make the move. The death of complacency is the death of poverty of the mind.

Accepting poverty, or anything less than being the best version of yourself, is ultimately a selfish act. It deprives the world of what you may have contributed, as well as siphoning resources from those who are genuinely unable to care for themselves.

GOD EXPECTS YOUR SUCCESS

If you are a person of faith, your success is not just needed by society; God expects it as a return on his investment in you:

> So take the bag of gold from him and give it to the one who has ten bags. For whoever has will be given more, and they will have an abundance. Whoever does not have, even what they have will be taken from them. And throw that worthless servant outside, into the darkness, where there will be weeping and gnashing of teeth.
>
> —Matthew 25:28-30(NIV)

Why do people put money into retirement accounts? To grow an investment which will return a profit while they no longer work. Many plant and tend gardens to reap a harvest once the plants reach maturity. In the same way, God made you as fertile soil and then planted the seeds of dreams and desires into you. Embedded in each of us is a level of mental and physical capacity each is responsible for nurturing and growing.

> *If the last thing God did in your life was to put you on earth with your innate capacity, He should expect a return on what He invested in you. However, there is much more available to everyone—we all have the opportunity to build on the foundation we have and to seek God's direction in our lives.*
> —**Paul Huber** *Killing Complacency*

Walking through the Parable of the Talents illustrates what God expects of everyone. (Matt 25:14-30) The parable starts with a wealthy landowner preparing for a long journey by entrusting portions of his wealth to his servants according to their ability—clearly, God gave us a range of abilities, and He is expecting results in proportion to the abilities invested.

Note the landowner going off for a long journey. While God is involved in our day to day, He puts the responsibility on us to execute the mission He prepared for us.

Upon his return, the landowner finds the two most capable managers were able to double the amount entrusted to them, and as a reward, gives them more work managing more of his estate. Just like today's business world, the reward for a job well done is more work and more responsibility.

For the employee who proved his lack of worth through inaction, the result was brutal—all he had been given was taken from him, given to the employee with the most, and he was cast into outer darkness.

> *No matter how little you feel God has given you by way of ability, you are called upon to use it well and to make the most of it.*
> —**Paul Huber** *Killing Complacency*

The result of not fulfilling God's full calling on your life is that the rewards intended for you will be given to another. If you are given much, and you are a good steward of what you have been given, more will be added unto you. Why do some accumulate so much while others are destitute? Perhaps, it's due in part to

COMPLACENCY

the failure of those with little, to be responsible with what little they do have. Undoubtedly, those who are poor financial stewards spend all of their money on junk rather than furthering their ability to earn, but instead merely fulfill their lust for accumulation.

WHAT DO YOU LOVE?

All too frequently, someone claims the Bible says money is the root of all evil—it does not. It does say, "But those who want to be rich fall into temptation, a trap, and many foolish and harmful desires, which plunge people into ruin and destruction. For the love of money is a root of all kinds of evil, and by craving it, some have wandered away from the faith and pierced themselves with many pains." 1 Timothy 6:9-10 (HCSB) Are you in love with money, or is it merely a tool for your success and furthering your calling?

While food is necessary for sustenance, our love of food may lead to being overweight or even corpulent. It's not the fault of the food itself but rather our attitude and behavior toward it. If we love fitness more than food, we will do what it takes to make food our slave rather than our master. Similarly, if we want godly success, we will make money our servant and God our master.

The love of money leads to all sorts of foolish decisions—like pursuing get rich quick schemes. Discerning the difference between foolish schemes and emerging opportunities can be hard—anything you don't understand can look like a scheme.

If you don't want to take the risk of discerning between a scheme and an emerging opportunity, it's relatively easy to identify recent salaries for various college degrees and trade school certifications and to look at trends, like the increased use of technology and automation. Though it's easy to see where the demand is (and is heading), it can take years of schooling for a person to help meet the demand—there is no easy path to success, just some are more or less hard. Some efforts provide small returns, while others provide greater returns.

CALCULATING THE RETURN ON GIVING

Whether you are a person of faith or not, consider tithing (giving 10% of your income) to the place that provides you with inspiration. As a believer, this gives back to God a portion of what He has given you the ability to produce. As they say, God knows that if He can get it through you, he will give it to you.

Regardless of your religious beliefs, giving allows your mind to believe you have sufficient abundance and the capacity to produce more. In addition to the positive feelings generated by giving, it unleashes your mind to produce more income.

Though giving in order to receive more seems selfish, the upward spiral of receiving more means there is more to give. More earning results in more spending—

helping those who produce goods and services, but more earning also means more giving—helping those in need and the spiritual leaders who provide valuable insight and guidance.

SPECIAL BONUS OFFER
GO TO
pauljhuber.com/kc-bonuses
to download exclusive
content for readers of
Killing Complacency.

CHAPTER FOUR

THE HERO'S JOURNEY

The most pervasive theme in literature is the hero's journey. The gist of this theme is the hero is called (or shoved) out of his safe home for an adventure. Instead of success, the hero succumbs to temptation and ends up in the abyss. Only after realizing the wisdom of his mentor, he is able to transform, atone for his failures, and returns to where he should have been. Despite the seemingly formulaic nature of the hero's journey template, our minds are hard-wired for entertainment or enlightenment from each unique variant of the hero's journey.

Perhaps the great universality for audiences is the reassurance that no matter where you are in your journey, it's never too late to change course—to pivot just like the hero of the story.

> *You are the hero of your story—choose to make the pivot to the most successful version of yourself.*
> —**Paul Huber** *Killing Complacency*

JUST CAN'T WAIT TO BE KING

The Lion King starts the hero's journey with young Simba excited for the future power he will enjoy as king—to the point when he sings he, *Just Can't Wait to be King.* Simba fell for the trap of desiring power without responsibility, perks without paying the price, and strength without a workout.

Thanks to a little push from his uncle Scar, Simba runs away unprepared to assume his responsibility as king after his father's early death. Completing the hero's journey, Simba returns to take his rightful place of leadership and reverses Scar's mismanagement of his territory. In the end, Simba builds up his strength, earns his position of power, and shows responsibility in managing his territory.

Providing biblical contrast, the Prophet Samuel anointed David as King of Israel long before he became king. God chose David, the smallest and most unlikely of his brothers, to become king when he was just a teenager. Instead of crowing about his future role, he simply returned to tending sheep. (1 Samuel 16)

The first-born sons of nobility, and a select few others, have advanced notice of their expected role in life. Most of us though, lack the slightest clue about where we are going; the result for many is, rather than striving for future greatness, we ride wherever the wind takes us.

Andres Pira was on such a path—one that looked like it could end with an early death from excessive alcohol use. Pira's fate turned when a friend sent him a book rather than money. Recently kicked out of his apartment, Andres was living on a Thai beach—and instead of money to meet his daily needs, he received an electronic copy of *The Secret*—not even something he could burn to keep warm. (Byrne, 2006)

Through skeptically applying what he read, Andres shifted his mindset on numerous fronts. He stopped blaming his circumstances on others, and recognized they were the results of the choices he made. He shifted from visualizing his next high to visualizing his next success. After his shift of mindset, and lots of work, he wrote *From Homeless to Billionaire.* * That's right—by shifting his mindset from the short-term to long-term, and his work ethic from getting by to thriving—Andres moved from nothing to substantial wealth. (Pira, 2019)

* *Andres is worth about 1 billion Thai baht, the equivalent of about 33 million US dollars—still a substantial sum, but worthy of the asterisk.*

Rather than simply having their dreams of success granted with all of the attendant pleasures, all of the "heroes" described throughout this book had to move from having little, to being responsible with what they did have, to amassing great wealth and power.

SMALL BEGINNINGS

It's an all too human tendency to excuse our lack of progress by saying others have gifts we lack. While there is undeniable variation in stature and mental capacity, far more of the variation in *outcomes* is the result of what a given person does with what they have.

Viewed through the lens of the fixed mindset, the story of David is just about how God can act through an ordinary man. The fixed mindset would tell you David killed Goliath and eventually became king of Israel, simply because God chose him to be the pointy end of His spear. David had something available only to him because of God.

Viewed through the lens of the growth mindset, David's story is about how he worked with God to be sharpened into a spear. Observing with a growth mindset, David is an example of how a godly person can grow and succeed. Though God chose David for a specific set of missions, his journey is something from which anyone can learn.

Shortly after being anointed King elect, David was called upon to play soothing music for the current king, Saul. Clearly, David was already building his skill set by practicing the lyre, just like many American children would be practicing the piano. The result of this first skill was the opportunity to observe the workings of the royal court long before the start of his role as king. (1 Samuel 16:14-22)

Long before he knew his job was to kill a giant, David was a responsible and aggressive shepherd. He undoubtedly "killed" countless trees and boulders as he practiced his slingshot skills—keeping busy during the quiet times of shepherding. When bears and lions eventually found the flock hoping for an easy snack, David used his mad slingshot skills to kill them.

On the day of the epic battle—one still mentioned thousands of years later—David brought the ancient equivalent of a gun to a knife fight. In pleading his case for permission to fight the giant, David recited his successes against the beasts of the field.

David didn't rush into the field of battle, merely hoping God would be with him. Instead, David trusted in his experience *and* in the prompting and protection of God in the moment. (1 Samuel 17) While the situation was not exactly like previous experiences, David knew it was a reasonable comparison to his current level of experience.

God's gift was not in guiding the stone to Goliath's skull. God's gift was in the preparation David had as he learned to use the slingshot. God's gift was in what most people would consider the bad days of shepherding, when a lion or bear would snatch a sheep for a late-night snack, and David would have to kill a real animal rather than pretending to kill the targets he had been using.

> *God's gifts are often the challenges*
> *meant to prepare us... the things we*
> *typically complain about.*
> —**Paul Huber** *Killing Complacency*

Choosing David as the future king demonstrated that even the "runt of the litter" could succeed through the combination of God's presence and his own hard work.

David didn't have a fairy godmother or a genie on his side; instead, he had the creator of hard work and of the natural laws governing the processes of growth.

GROWTH

David's small beginnings are analogous to so many other successful people. Arnold Schwarzenegger doesn't have any special bodybuilder or Governator DNA. Instead, a scrawny, young Arnold chose to try bodybuilding—working out several times each day and eating massive amounts of protein. Arnold's time in the gym was not aimlessly trying different machines; instead, he was applying what he learned in books and magazines about bodybuilding—experimenting with the tried and true methods as well as new ideas of his own.

Just like every other bodybuilder, Arnold spent about a decade building his massive physique. Just like every other "overnight success," Arnold spent around a decade growing and preparing before he achieved significant notoriety.

In *Quitter: Closing the Gap Between Your Day Job and Your Dream Job*, author and speaker Jon Acuff described his own move from obscurity working at a typical day job, to earning a living writing and speaking. For years, his Monday mornings felt like the equivalent of Superman covering his costume with his Clark Kent disguise and heading back to reporting. After feeling alive during his weekends traveling to speak at events, Acuff returned to his cubicle. (Acuff, 2011)

Certainly, some need to create a path from their day job to an external dream job—to be the best sort of quitter. However, for many more, a simple perspective and attitude shift is necessary. For still others, molding a role and a career trajectory to fit their desires is the best answer.

Chapter 10 challenges the broken, misguiding conventional thinking about passion, purpose, and calling. Addressing how you think about your employment—as a job, a career, or a calling, may be sufficient to bring about new energy to your day job. If you lack passion for your job, it may be only that perspective and proficiency are lacking.

Between the boredom of the mundane, repetitive tasks, and the distress of the currently unachievable, is the peak performance zone, according to psychologists. Rather than distress, we experience eustress—the good stress that gets work done and makes life enjoyable.

My career path (for my day job) is increasingly rare in the modern era—I have been with one employer since graduating college over 20 years ago. However, with a single employer, I have had numerous roles, allowing me to grow and stretch myself. The times when I have been happiest have been those where I have been able to be proactive in selecting my role to play to my strengths, and then continuing to refine it to best allocate work based on the shared strengths of me and my team.

I'm not saying everyone can always work on what they are absolutely the best at, or necessary efforts can be neglected because nobody excels at it. However, most people should spend the majority of their time working on either where they are already proficient or where they desire to be proficient.

While most books are about or created by the outliers of our society, they are, perhaps, not the best example of a healthy career path for those who are not outliers. The healthiest examples are those who continually grow within their chosen field, adapt to emerging technology and processes, and never give up learning.

The quickening evolution of technology rapidly exposes the engineers who maintain their edge, and those who were last sharpened years before in college. As my employer worked through a wave of retirements, maybe 10% will be noticeably missed due to their experience leaving the organization, and at least 20% should have left or been fired much sooner. The remaining approximately 70% are capable but easily replaced by a less expensive new graduates—which is a shame because they had the opportunity to be just as good as the top tier employees.

> *Not everyone can be an outlier, but everyone can commit to continual growth.*
> —**Paul Huber** *Killing Complacency*

THE COMPOUND EFFECT

Just as investing in your retirement account compounds over time, investing in yourself compounds over time. As John Maxwell says, "consistency compounds." Just as gaining muscle (or fat) requires repeated activity aligned with the direction of the desired (or undesired) outcome, your outcomes are the compounded results of your decisions—healthy or unhealthy, good or bad, helpful or unhelpful. (Maxwell J. , 2019)

The current state of your knowledge, bank accounts, or health is not who you are today; it's the accumulated residual of who you were previously. The person you are today has the opportunity to choose who you want to be tomorrow. (Byrne, 2006)

> *You are who you chose to be. You*
> *become who you choose to be.*
> —**Paul Huber** *Killing Complacency*

If you choose the path of the fixed mindset—avoiding effort and challenges, then your results will be the life of the mediocre and the miserable. However, choosing the growth mindset, pursuing challenges at the peak of your current ability (or just beyond), allows your abilities to compound.

The extraordinarily successful typically exert extraordinary effort to achieve their results—becoming deliberately unbalanced. However, diligence in your daily endeavors delivers dividends. The basic level of compounding does not require 100-hour workweeks or neglecting your family. What it does require, though, is moving beyond your fear of change. It requires discerning helpful from hateful feedback—and taking the right action. It requires giving up the sedating for the strengthening.

The Compound Effect, quite simply, is everyday choices and habits accumulating into accrued bene-fits or accrued problems. Food and exercise routines accumulate into health and fitness or sickness and weakness. Aligning habits and choices to your ambi-tions and dreams is the only way to have a chance of realizing them. Establishing good habits and useful skills builds momentum to achieve your ambitions. (Hardy, 2010)

> *Don't despise small beginnings.*
>   *Zechariah 4:10*

SPECIAL BONUS OFFER
GO TO
pauljhuber.com/kc-bonuses
to download exclusive
content for readers of
Killing Complacency.

CHAPTER FIVE

WHAT IS YOUR TRAJECTORY?

WHAT'S YOUR VECTOR, VICTOR?

In the fast-paced world of air traffic control, the single word *vector* is the shorthand method of discussing the heading and velocity of the aircraft. For example, a pilot may ask for a vector to the airport, or a controller may ask a pilot for their current vector. Of course, in the classic parody *Airplane,* Leslie Nielson asked, "what's your vector, Victor," providing hilarious alliteration and rhyming.

A pilot departing from Los Angeles with just a few degrees difference in the heading of their vector might land in either New York or Miami. Similarly, in our own lives, choosing a trajectory toward the success we want is critical for achieving the results we want.

Our trajectory may be as easy to measure as the vector of an airplane, or hard to measure and predict as next week's weather. While the weather forecaster may know a polar vortex is on the way, the exact snowfall and temperatures are dependent upon the movement of multiple air masses and weather systems.

The trajectory of our health can be easy to see at times as we gain or lose muscle or fat. Or it can be harder to spot, like the negligible, initial outward symptoms of smoking or our mental wellbeing. The trajectory of our financial wellbeing can be as quantifiable as our net-worth; or as hidden as failing to invest in our ability to continue earning. The former being a well-known financial equation, and the latter only being evident when we are unable to make a good living with our current skill level.

Making success your goal and subordinating your actions to your goal, means most of your decisions will better serve the goal. And though one approach to success may not lead to the victory the way you want, maintaining focus on success over the form it takes, will give you the power to pivot to the right opportunity.

MAINTAINING YOUR VECTOR

Maintaining a vector toward success can be a messy operation. Some may see an "overnight success" and assume getting there is as easy as it looked, or it really was a simple direct vector from novice to master. The reality is: the successful often spend years learning from their failures, mediocre successes, and even unexpected glimmers of success. Through the ups and downs though, there is a relentless push to their desired outcome. Those who study "overnight successes" realize most are actually a decade in the making. This is true from entertainment to entrepreneurship.

> *Continually pushing toward your goals is the only way to have any meaningful chance of success.*
> —**Paul Huber** *Killing Complacency*

The guys in *Dumb and Dumber* may be excited by a one in a million chance, and the lottery feeds on people hoping for the non-zero odds of winning. However, such odds do not lead to a financially stable retirement or success in life. Having meaningful odds of winning requires consistent effort in the direction of success.

From Steve Martin's comedy, to Arnold Schwarzenegger's bodybuilding, to Amazon, all notable successes are rooted in years of perseverance. In the case of infomercial purveyor of gadgets, Ron Popeil, his success came after generations who toiled in the kitchen gadget business. (Martin, 2007) (Schwarzenegger, 2012) (Gladwell, 2009)

Again, consistent effort compounds. While years may go by before the full reward of consistency is realized, the daily compounding moves the consistent incrementally closer to their goal. Consistent effort compounding may come in the form of incrementally larger successes or more painfully and realistically; it may come through a mix of success and failure. As they say, sometimes you succeed, other times you learn.

Steve Martin spent years performing magic, playing the banjo, and building a comedy routine which eventually landed him on the Tonight Show with Johnny Carson, and on-stage in giant arenas. Watching videos of Martin from the 1970s and 1980s, one might imagine his simplistic, slapstick comedy just happened... nothing could be further from reality. The routine was the result of spending a decade honing his craft in front of small audiences. After his success in comedy, his prior experience facilitated his pivot to movies. The existing notoriety and comedic timing formed a foundation upon which he could build the next phase of his career.

TRIALS OF MANY KINDS

The innate wiring of our brains expects clean and neat narratives to explain the successes and failures we see or experience. However, trials of many kinds come our way. Some are the natural consequences of our own actions, or our own failure to have proper oversight of those we trusted to help us. Some trials are the accumulated results of a society's irrational exuberance, and others are disasters from nature. Some trials defy any explanation. Believers, though, are promised trials: John 16:33, James 1:2-4.

Regardless of the source of our trials, all we can control is our reaction.

> *If you are going to go through it, you might as well go through it well.*
> —**Paul Huber** *Killing Complacency*

Regardless of the source of our trials, the best result is to become stronger. You may feel like you are being punished, held back, or denied the rightful fruits of your efforts. However, the answer to any of those is to become strong enough to avoid experiencing the same trial over again.

As Napoleon Hill said, "I have also discovered that there comes with every experience of temporary defeat, and every failure and every form of adversity, the seed of an equivalent benefit." (Hill, 2012)

LIFE FOCUS

Though it's not always easy to measure the vector of your life, your life focus should be easy to spot—and manage. As Jerry Foster discusses in *Life Focus,* the first step is to define success in each area of your life, and then work relentlessly toward your definition of success. As a man, I have many roles: husband, father, son, brother, employee, leader, volunteer, etc. (Foster, 2004)

If I fail to keep my body healthy, my spiritual being focused, or my family in balance, it makes no difference how my business runs. A deterioration of my body due to neglect means I am unable to operate well in any of the above areas. (White, 2017)

You are the CEO of your own life, as Brian Tracy explains it. As the leader of a one-person business, it's your responsibility to sustain your business just as a company's leader is required to help sustain the business they lead.

Consider the positive benefits of a life focused on sustainably providing value to the world—where sustained profitability provides for sustained and ever-improving service.

BE YOUR OWN CEO

I don't know about you, but my boss asks me to do things I would rather not do. My boss is demanding, and the higher you go up the ladder, the bosses get tougher. I once heard senior leaders at my company refer to the annual planning process as the "annual crucifixion before [the CEO]." That sounds brutal!

Imagine enforcing the same brutal high expectations on yourself as a tough boss would. Not perfectionist, self-loathing high expectations. Not the irrational expectations and snarky feedback of a bad boss. Imagine not just the annual, work-related personal growth plan you have to write for your boss, but also a plan including all areas of your life – body, being, balance, and business. A plan taking reasonable next steps to the level of growth you want and need.

Imagine assigning yourself the necessary and mundane tasks as well as the glorious and exiting ones.

This is especially true for anyone with a side-hustle or self-employed job. The *War of Art* describes overcoming the resistance inside of each of us—especially the artist and writer. Moving from an amateur artist to professional requires professional behaviors and structures—even going as far as having a Monday morning status meeting with yourself. (Pressfield, 2002)

Do the things you don't want to do (but know you need to do), in order to have the things you want to have. As the CEO of You Inc., be the boss who gets the most out of people through positive motivation.

SPECIAL BONUS OFFER
GO TO
pauljhuber.com/kc-bonuses
to download exclusive
content for readers of
Killing Complacency.

CHAPTER SIX

THE GROWTH MINDSET AND INFINITE OPPORTUNITY

> *The world has ample abundance for everyone—do your part to earn your portion and encourage everyone else to do the same.*
> —**Paul Huber** *Killing Complacency*

THE ABUNDANCE OF THIS WORLD

Did you know aluminum, the metal so inexpensive it's used to package your sugar water or fermented barley water, your gum, and your leftovers, was once more valuable than the gold used in your expensive jewelry? The history of unlocking this remarkably abundant substance was revealed to me in *Abundance: The Future is Better than you Think*, a book high on Bill Gate's recommended reading list. Unlocking the abundance of aluminum is just one example of human ingenuity unlocking the abundance of this world.

Through the proliferation of electricity and public water systems, we have eliminated some of the most time-consuming burdens our ancestors had to deal with—though they have not been eliminated for everyone. The abundance unleashed by these inno-vations accelerated the industrial revolution and the information revolution that followed.

Current projections show that through the growth of modern technology and economic expansion, extreme poverty according to our current definition, could be eliminated as early as 2030. The growth benefits everyone, and we are not at risk of running out of anything.

The abundance of money in this world has no prac-tical limit. NONE. While many consider one person gaining money is the result of another losing it, nothing could be further from the truth. One person gives another money because what they receive in return has more value than the money. And the product or service sold costs the seller less than the money received. The differences between cost and price is not simply profit, but it represents the productive output captured by the transaction —the more productive output in an economy, the more value created by its members.

While our monetary system is not the textbook ideal system, it's close enough to understand the abun-dance of money in our society. With an ideal monetary system, the supply of money would correlate with the productive output of the economy it represents. In other words, roughly, as the output of the economy increases, the money available to those producing the output increases. BOOM. There is no shortage of money—only a shortage of those willing and able to

do what it takes to get the money, and a shortage of effort in the right direction to earn the money.

The modern education system produces a shortage of people well equipped to earn money, but we don't lack the availability of money. We have a shortage of people who handle money well, but we don't lack available money.

Though *How an Economy Grows and Why it Crashes* ends with, perhaps, an overworked analogy to describe the process of the crash, it begins with a simple analogy of economic growth:

> *Three men are stranded on an island, and each one has to spend a full day to catch one fish to feed himself for a day.*
>
> *After a while, one of the three goes hungry for a day in order to invent a fishing machine which allows him to catch a fish in only half a day — freeing him up to spend more time further increasing his productivity or building a better shelter.*

As the analogy continues, the little island economy continues to grow and flourish, and more people begin to arrive. Cycles of investing rather than consuming continue to allow the islanders to increase productivity. Some of the increases are consumed and enjoyed, but many are reinvested into growing the economy and improving the standard of living for all.

GOD'S ABUNDANCE

For people of faith, the abundance is not just of this world, but also the next—and the God who created this abundant world is active in both what is seen and what is unseen.

Too many of my fellow believers have given up on the abundance of this world, and are simply waiting for the abundance of the next. However, the Parable of the Talents demonstrated we are not to simply hope for abundance, but that we are called to create it. Success is not found in burying your treasure but in multiplying it through your effort.

> *The truth that there are more important things than money was corrupted by those who seek to mute your ambition or excuse their own lack of drive and results.*
> —**Paul Huber** *Killing Complacency*

Loving your family is important—but feelings do not put food on the table (or buy the table and dining room). Time volunteering and attending church builds community and allows you to learn, but without making money as well, there is nothing to fund the mission of the church. It's worthwhile to care for the poor, but feelings do not buy food or fund programs to help them.

If you care for your family, your church, or the poor, then you need to make prudent decisions on how you invest your time, and treasure in each. In fact, sometimes, the best investment may be in caring for or improving yourself. You may require more rest or better self-care, or you may need more improved skills for your work or personal life. Sometimes, your best gift to others is your own health and fitness.

Seeking God's abundance is not all rainbows and unicorns, though. The process of building our ability to reap the available abundance can be more painful than the aftermath of a trip to the gym, and more glorious than winning Mr. Universe.

THE GET OFF YOUR BUTT DOCTRINE

When it comes to money and the church, the spectrum of beliefs is broad. At one extreme is the "prosperity doctrine," arguing God wants you to be prosperous in proportion to your giving, while at the other extreme are sects where the priests take a vow of poverty. If you are a believer, forget for a moment about how much or how little God wants you to have in possessions and cash money, and instead consider how much he wants you to work.

If you are a believer or curious about what the Bible says about work, I want you to do a bit of work right now and look up these passages. In fact, do some extra work to explore the context to know that the cited verses are representative of the message being conveyed.

- Genesis 2:15-17

- Proverbs 6:6-11

- Proverbs 21:25-26

- 2 Thessalonians 3:6-12

- Colossians 3:22-24

The bottom line of these passages is:

- The first thing God asked a human to do is work.

- He is warning us against the natural consequences of laziness.

- As early as the first century, the church struggled with some people not producing at the level they should—perhaps turning the safety net into a hammock.

- When we work, it should represent our best effort—as if it was for God himself.

- We are here to work and to do it well. There is no escape from work, only cycles of exertion and recovery.

THE DICHOTOMY OF SELF-SUFFICIENCY

The mindset of rugged individualism and the myth of the self-made man resulted in too many who were unwilling or unable to ask for help when it was needed. Some of the most successful "self-made men" had a less famous partner whose strengths counterbalanced their weaknesses. Steve Jobs was the front-man selling Apple, while Steve Wozniak was the lead engineering genius who made the early products work. Bill Gates partnered with Paul Allen, and Warren Buffett with Charlie Munger, even Wild Bill had Charlie Utter.

The dichotomy, however, is that excessive individualism has given way to those who are unable to get out of bed in the morning without the village experge-factor rousing them.

The ideal state is what Steven Covey refers to as interdependence. The first three of his *7 Habits of Highly Effective People* facilitate independence, and the next three facilitate interdependence rather than codependence. Interdependence allows the whole to be more effective than the sum of its parts, whereas codependence brings everyone down to the least common denominator.

Learning to tie your own shoes builds independence. Knowing enough not to start DIY brain surgery shows the interdependence of our society.

EMBRACING AVERAGE

The good news for the average reader is the abundance of this world is not out of reach. The amazing results we like to attribute to genius are typically the result of hard work performed in obscurity.

By attributing the success of others to some genetic or God-given gift, too many of us are looking for an excuse for our own lack of progress. By moving the responsibility outside of our locus of control, we place the blame on others rather than taking the action we need to.

Perhaps one of the best examples of an alleged child prodigy was the classical composer Wolfgang Amadeus Mozart. In *Peak*, Anders Erickson dissected this alleged prodigy. Rather than finding an actual prodigy, he found a pedagogue father—someone who studied the musical education process.

The elder Mozart was focused on training his children in music—teaching them first to recognize notes and then how to write music. The younger Mozart became a good musician at an early age because of an early start, and constant training from an expert teacher. His gift was his situation, not his genetics or a divine touch nobody else could have.

Centuries later, Thomas Edison's mother, exasperated by the school system labeling him as slow, took to educating him herself. His teachers were probably right—but the deliberate effort he applied to problem solving, helped him lead the teams of inventors who created the early version of many of our modern convenience.

Edison's one-time employee and eventual nemesis, Nicola Tesla, had a far more developed and seemingly

intuitive understanding of electricity and successfully created the initial version of the distribution system we have today.

Why was Edison more celebrated and Tesla more obscure (until Elon Musk named a car company after him)? Because despite his average (or below) intellect, he had learned to promote his work better and to manage the teams, who were applying the 99% perspiration required to achieve his 1% inspiration.

When I visited the Ford-Edison winter estates in Fort Meyers, Florida, I marveled at the lab he had established there. It was amazing to learn that early incandescent bulbs used non-metallic filaments and Edison's team was searching the world for the best option. Within his laboratory, he had row after row of workbenches—I could only imagine the sweatshop environment created by the warm Florida sun.

At my modern American engineering job, the team dons their beach attire when the air conditioning breaks and lab temperatures rise above 80 degrees. One day, as I entered an overheated lab, one of my teammates was wearing a tank top undershirt rather than his usual professional attire… a far cry from Edison's breeze cooled lab from the days before air conditioning.

There are endless examples of average people accomplishing the extraordinary. That's the bottom-line message of *Peak*… through purposeful and deliberate practice, *anyone* can accomplish far more than they would have expected. Of course, the competition for the position of best in the world is fierce. Olympic athletes and the best musicians need to put in 10,000 hours of practice (much of it painful, deliberate practice) in order to be competitive. It's this application of deliberate practice that makes them better than those who showed a spark of ability but stopped their pursuit earlier.

Instead of lamenting whatever gifts you think you were not given, do as Liz Forkin Bannon recommends in *Beginners Pluck:* own your average. Remember contentment without complacency? Be content with how you were made, and your experiences up to this moment. Be realistic about what you can do, whether you believe you have an innate gift or a developed skill. Be intentional and relentless, though, in moving from where you are to where you desire to go.

As James pointed out (James 5:17)—Elijah was just a man. David was just a man. Schwarzenegger only pretended to be part cyborg. We are all just men and women. Achieving great things is a matter of being willing to start small, apply deliberate effort along the right trajectory and, as needed, massive action.

GROWING BEYOND AVERAGE

Whether or not we feel called to our work, our survival often requires our work. Our desires to consume the abundance provided by this world often drives us to work more. So, if we are working anyway, why not work the best we can? If we are working anyway, why not use the time to become better—becoming more valuable and able to receive more in exchange for our time and ability. If we are going to work anyway, why not move the bar on what constitutes average performance.

The growth *Mindset* tells us we have far more ability to grow if, instead of assuming we have a fixed set of "gifts," we believe we have an unlimited potential to grow. (Dweck, 2006) The tools of purposeful and deliberate practice from *Peak* provide the mechanisms for taking average "gifts" to accomplish your mission. (Erickson & Pool, 2006) The most amazing gift available is available to everyone—living in the modern world. This gift allows anyone to first reap from the available abundance and then to share it for the benefit of others.

At work, solicit feedback on what you can do better. To go further, create an environment where everyone is good at giving and receiving feedback in a way that elicits growth rather than hostility. While athletes and performers have the luxury of spending hundreds of hours in practice for every hour of game time, the rest of us need to practice while we perform.

Those who persist in the fixed mindset see little more than pain in the challenges of life, envy the success of others, and ultimately achieve less than what they could—less than what they were placed on earth to do.

By contrast, those with a growth mindset are able to grow from the effort and adversity they face, find inspiration and education from the success of others, and achieve far more than they would have with the fixed mindset.

For a believer, the pain of adversity is soothed by knowing God works all things together for good. (Romans 8:28) The secular equivalent is Napoleon Hill's notion that every negative experience has a seed of something good in it. The growth mindset says, even though something undeniably bad happens, it's my responsibility to choose my response, and use the experience for my growth rather than allowing it to trap me.

> *It's OK to be not OK—but it's not OK to not do anything about it.*
> *—Paul Huber Killing Complacency*

Getting knocked down by the challenges of life is normal. Having the challenges drive you to being not OK is OK... but staying there is not OK. Imagine having your arm broken—severely broken, not just a hairline fracture—but then not doing anything to have it set back to the way it should be, and allowed to heal. Your arm could end up useless. In the same way, if you are not OK, the best thing to do is get the right kind of help or to have the right long-term compensation strategy.

With the growth mindset, the "average" person can grow beyond average. With a growth mindset, you may not choose to climb to the pinnacle of your field, but you can choose to move beyond average with little additional effort.

If we all choose the growth mindset, then we can move average to a higher level of achievement.

SPECIAL BONUS OFFER
GO TO
pauljhuber.com/kc-bonuses
to download exclusive
content for readers of
Killing Complacency.

CHAPTER SEVEN

KNOW YOUR ENEMY

> *We may say that to know yourself and to know your enemy; you will gain victory a hundred times out of a hundred.*
>
> —**Sun Tzu** *The Art of War*

ACHIEVING SUCCESS IS WAR

Every path in life is a battle—a battle to survive or a battle to thrive. If you are going to fight—and you must—you might as well fight for success and not merely survival. You may believe your competition is your enemy.

However, they merely provide a benchmark—your opportunity to differentiate yourself in some way.

THE ENEMY IS ALL AROUND YOU

For the believer, the devil personifies the enemy. His job is to steal, kill, and destroy. He drops temptation into your life—pulling you off track. He saps your drive—keeping you from getting on the track. He puts you into overdrive—making you jump the track.

COMPLACENCY

Too fast or too slow, he wins. To the left or to the right, he wins.

Whether you believe in the existence of the devil or not, the systems of the world do an equally good job of working against us. The fundamental needs of our survival cost money. The needs and wants of our families cost money too. As a result, we spend most of our waking lives trading our time for the money we need and want to fulfill our lifestyles.

Marketers spend their time on making us want what they have. We want to buy the shoes so we can be like Mike—or LeBron or Steph. We want the house, the car, and the big screen TV. We want the hot woman [or man], or at least the chance to imagine being with them.

Pleasure is fleeting. It drives us to mistakenly choose lifestyle over personal growth and expenses over investments that produce a return. When investing is a priority, the long-term gains can accrue to a much greater lifestyle later in life.

At the business of You Inc., include the corporate budget line items of "Research and Development" (R&D) and "Training." Include them for the same reasons corporations do—to increase and sustain value. Use the budget to create educational opportunities like filling your queue of audiobook listening at Drivetime University (a very low tuition school where the tuition is only the cost of books and class time combines with commuting time).

Money and the things it buys becomes addictive, which makes it hard to allocate time and income to personal R&D and training. The new cellphone is more attractive than the training course. Netflix is more attractive than the book that will build your skills—and the cycle continues.

Not that gadgets or leisure are bad—they are very important. The problem is the proportion and the priority. The solution is setting priorities and living out a schedule reflecting your priorities.

The allure of daily distractions diminishes when you are excited about your career path, and work to move from where you are today to where you want to go.

THE ENEMY IS WITHIN YOU

Regardless of what happens around us or to us, each of us is responsible for how we respond—or don't respond. Sometimes the best response is inaction—like declining to escalate the fight with your spouse. However, all too often, the easy answer is inaction, but the beneficial answer is action. Even wrong action is better than inaction, when the result is progress toward a goal and learning along the way.

COMPLACENCY IS THE ENEMY

Complacency tells us we are good enough where we are. It tells us to stop striving, to embrace the suck, to not even bother to try. Complacency allows us to long for more, without the action to earn the more that we want. Complacency disguises itself as noble content-ment but drags us to inaction.

Complacency though, is just one of the enemies within, slowing us from the progress we are here to make.

AVOIDING PAIN IS THE ENEMY

We are hard-wired to avoid pain. Pulling back from the hot stove or the unexpected pinprick is completely reasonable. Not jumping when stabbed by a nurse with a hypodermic needle requires mental focus and well-managed expectations. More challenging, though, is willingly enduring the pain of the intense physical exertion required to build muscles. For many, the psychological pain of putting ourselves in an uncom-fortable situation is enough to dissuade us from doing it. From not asking out that cute girl to not asking the bank for the massive loan that will build our business, our fear of rejection keeps us from even trying.

To succeed, you need to become comfortable with being uncomfortable. Leaning into discomfort in one area, like exercising, may make it easier to deal with the discomfort of another area, but it does not replace it.

> *Achieving growth in any area requires discomfort.*
> —**Paul Huber** *Killing Complacency*

INERTIA IS THE ENEMY

Just as the inertia of physical objects at rest wants to keep them at rest, the inertia of your current situation wants to keep you there. Typically, only when a person's situation becomes completely unbearable does action ensue. When it's short of unbearable, the current situation is familiar and relatively comforting.

The good news about inertia is, once you are in motion, you will tend to stay in motion. Like a freight train going at full speed, it will take incredible effort for an abrupt stop. Though everyone should know that the inertia of a train is nothing to mess with, somehow every year people still die taking on trains. Everyone should know better than to take on the inertia of your success.

RESISTANCE IS THE ENEMY

Like friction, though, the persistent force of resistance will exert continual pressure to slow and stop you.

> *Resistance is relentless in its opposition.*
> —**Paul Huber** *Killing Complacency*

Immediately after overcoming the inertia of inaction, the resistance begins. It will tell you that you were foolish to start and you should cut your losses early. Resistance will tell you that you are not good enough or pull you into distractions and procrastination.

Resistance will pull you off mission with a thousand other activities that are "good" but not conducive to meeting your goals.

Worst of all, resistance is the one force able to stop the completion of a project just before its finale—right before the inertia of the effort launches it into the world. When the book is due to the publisher; when it's time to send the app to the app store; when it's time to make the sales pitch to the big potential customer. (Pressfield, 2002)

THE ENEMY OF YOUR ENEMIES: DEFINITENESS OF PURPOSE

The enemy of inertia is definiteness of purpose. The enemy of resistance is definiteness of purpose. The salve for the pain of progress is definiteness of purpose. With a definite purpose, we will bear any burden, endure any pain, and persevere until our purpose is met.

Definiteness of purpose smells a lot like ambition— the drive to achieve the success God expects from you, and the world needs from you. However, a definite purpose defines the means of success. It moves from generalized ambition, to specified purpose. Chapter 10 resolves the myths associated with passion and purpose to clarify the mission of You Inc.

Being definite about your purpose causes your mind to find opportunities that align with your purpose. If you ever purchased a vehicle and then suddenly noticed how many similar cars are on the roads, the change was not the popularity of the vehicle, but you mind being primed to see that type of vehicle. Priming you mind for success through a definite purpose helps you see opportunities—instead of problems and obstacles.

SPECIAL BONUS OFFER
GO TO
pauljhuber.com/kc-bonuses
to download exclusive
content for readers of
Killing Complacency.

CHAPTER EIGHT

THE DEATH OF COMPLACENCY – PART 1

The fruit of complacency is a life less than it could be—less than God intended it to be. Like weeds in a garden, complacency chokes out the harvest we desire. Instead of fruit that benefits us, our family, our world, and our church, complacency produces nothing while taking up the limited space and nutrients available in the garden of life.

This is why the death of complacency should not feel like mourning the passing of what is comfortable, but the celebration of removing weeds from the garden of your life. Whether you need a funeral pyre or to burn the refuse, this chapter and the next one seek to kill complacency at the roots.

While complacency is fully an inside job, feelings of envy and guilt are hidden triggers of complacency. Masquerading as garden variety negative emotions, the pair seeks to limit our efforts and results by making us feel unworthy and undeserving of success. Actively overcoming feelings of envy and guilt is not just important for happiness; it's important for success.

By replacing complacency with responsible ambition, we change our habitual thoughts, which translate into our habitual feelings and actions. Because most of our feelings and actions are habitual, when complacency is dead, we are alive to pursue our purpose.

KILLING ENVY

> *Nobody's success is robbing your potential. There is enough wind in the harbor to sail more than one ship.*
> —*Scott Hagan (Hagan, 2019)*

T. Harv Eker learned the secrets to the millionaire mindset, including both a growth mindset and the death of envying those who have more than you do. By overcoming envy he made the first step to his success. (Eker, 2009)

Envy is probably the most insidious roots of complacency because it subtly drives more complacency and / or wrong behavior:

- Envy drives people to spread the fixed mindset—keeping those who might rise above in their place.
- Envy causes us, subconsciously, to put limits on our own achievement.
- Envy leads us to take shortcuts to "success" or accumulation.
- Envy tempts many into sin and crime.

Envy, the ultimate form of self-sabotage, typically hurts the envier, not the envied. When we envy others, we program our minds to believe their level of achievement or material possession is somehow wrong. Our mind, not wanting to have an internal conflict, consciously or subconsciously, believes achieving the same level for ourselves would be wrong and keeps us from it.

In those with a fixed mindset, envy causes them to see the success of others as a threat. Conversely, the success of others is an inspiration for those without envy and with a growth mindset. (Dweck, 2006)

All too often, envy leads to wrong behavior. Take a look at a few of the Ten Commandments from Exodus 20:14-17 (KJV):

> *Thou shalt not commit adultery. Thou shalt not steal.*
>
> *Thou shalt not bear false witness against thy neighbour.*
>
> *Thou shalt not covet thy neighbour's house, thou shalt not covet thy neighbour's wife, nor his manservant, nor his maidservant, nor his ox, nor his ass, nor any thing that is thy neighbour's.*

When we covet our neighbor's belongings or relationships—his wife, his ass, or his wife's assets, we open ourselves to adultery, theft, and deception. It's not that desiring something comparable is bad; the problem arises when we seek to take what someone else has or to acquire by lying, cheating, or stealing.

Even with commands against it, envy can be an insidious undercurrent in the church. When one member gets a nicer car, another thinks or says, "Just think about how the church could have benefited if they had the money instead."

The envy escalates, as pastors seem to be expected to take a vow of poverty instead of being paid according to the outcomes they produce. While some assuage their low pay with sayings like, "the outcome is more important than the income," just like a business, the pastors with the best outcomes deserve the best incomes. Those who effectively lead a congregation (or their part of one) and build a decent side hustle with activities like writing books or songs, are prudently building multiple streams of income—just like an effective entrepreneur.

Envy is easy. Getting results is much harder. When we see others being successful or reaping the results of their success, it's easy to think they don't deserve it or they cheated to get it. Typically, the results come from endless hours of practice and preparation. Wealthy entrepreneurs build a money-earning machine by assembling money-earning components—each piece, each employee bringing in a portion of the overall wealth.

Did you know it takes ten years (or more) to become an overnight success? Some of this is attributed to the

10,000-hour rule, which indicates how much deliberate practice is required to become world-class. (Gladwell, 2008) However, much of this time is also dedicated to building awareness and a network of supporters and promoters. Comedians like Jerry Seinfeld, Jim Gaffigan, and John Crist may burst into our awareness, but they first spent years honing their craft and hours practicing and tweaking their routines in front of smaller crowds, before we became aware of them and bought tickets to their shows.

Not only entertainers and athletes require years of building. Even businesses require significant time and effort to help them grow—years to build the critical mass necessary to grow and to become widely known.

I recently heard of a philanthropist couple that reflected on their ability to give, and recalled the time they had to sell their house to keep their fledgling business afloat. The result of their sacrifices—large and small—led to a thriving business and the ability to give generously in their later years.

We envy what seems easy for others to attain when we are unaware of the true struggle it took to achieve what they did. The thief turns to burglary when it seems easier than the honest alternative and when the legitimate routes to success seem unavailable. Unfortunately, the legitimate routes are cut off by nothing more than the wrong mindset and not by the reality of the situation.

Scooter Braun, who discovered pop stars including Justin Bieber, advises, "Stop counting other people's money." Rather than allowing envy to drive imprudent attempts at success, follow the path laid out for you. Follow the path that uses your interests, skills, and even your calling, to first bring value and then reap rewards. Have an impact in a way that brings a sustaining income.

KILLING GUILT

Similar to envy, guilt dampens our drive to succeed and can drive self-sabotage. In the case of guilt, rather than wishing we had more, we feel bad for what we do have. Both our own behaviors and the messages from our churches and the media drive this guilt.

First, our own behavior: it's easy to fail at being content and to attempt to buy our way to happiness by accumulating belongings—and debt. We buy bigger houses than we can afford, newer, better cars than our budget can bear, and more big-boy and big-girl toys than we ever need. Rather than accumulating knowledge and assets that build wealth, we build a debt load we can barely sustain. We should feel bad.

We should feel bad when we burden ourselves and our families with excessive debt. Well-used debt is a powerful tool to provide transportation and shelter with reasonable monthly payments. Best of all, a smartly used debt can be the right leverage to start or grow a business. Unfortunately, without the right sense of contentment, it's easy to use debt to satisfy short-term longings with the long-term consequences of high payments. (Kiyosaki, 2009)

Kill the guilt of excessive borrowing by learning to be content but not complacent. Build your earning power before spending more. Having margin in the budget for skill growth, investing, emergency expenses, and giving will make a world of difference in your life and, by extension, a difference in the world.

To see the extent to which America and the western world is better off, look no further than the news media, your social media feed, or your favorite charity's latest plea for money. The fixed mindset, envy, and guilt might tell you that our abundance is at their expense. Nothing could be further from the truth. Trading value for value—money for goods and services helps everyone involved in the process and spills out into benefits for the greater society.

> *In a business transaction, guilt should only arise if one party is cheating another—receiving value without providing the expected amount in return.*
> —**Paul Huber** *Killing Complacency*

The successes of the western world should not be a source of guilt or shame. Instead, it should be a model to help pull the rest of the world out of poverty. It's exciting to see some organizations, like the Institute for Faith, Work, and Economics (IFWE), are putting deliberate thought into moving from the resource-draining, dependency building handouts to self-sustaining business and economic programs. (For the Least of These, 2014) I desire that my book also helps in the process of moving people, especially those who feel they are the least of these; from complacency to contentment without complacency with responsible ambition—from feeling trapped to feeling freed—from drifting to a definite purpose.

From politicians to preachers, we hear about evil or excessive profits. Many assume a profit for one is a loss for another. However, economic growth and increased productivity is an important aspect of the economy—not simply greedy consumerism. (Schiff & Schiff, 2010) Profits are an indicator of the efficacy of a business, and losses are not a sign of a saintly business—losses cannot be sustained and lead to more people in misery looking for income to sustain their needs. (For the Least of These, 2014)

> *There is nothing wrong with profiting; only wrong ways to gain profit.*
> —**Paul Huber** *Killing Complacency*

One Sunday morning, my pastor was trying to encourage a robust offering and provided a mangled, out of context quote about profits being evil. It took me a while to cool down afterwards—I wanted to punch him in the throat (one of his favorite phrases), or at least just get up and walk out of service. After a few minutes, I just decided to hope he misspoke and to retain membership in the church (or not) based on his long-term presentation of the Gospel, including how to perceive profit.

Proverbs 11:1 (MSG) succinctly summarizes the biblical view of commerce and cheating, "God hates cheating in the marketplace; he loves it when business is aboveboard." God loves "honest scales" and "honest measures" in business. When gaining profit honestly, both the buyer and seller benefit, and the competitors have a fair shot at selling their goods or services.

While ethical profit is good, Habakkuk 11:9 warns those who build an empire on dishonesty, "Woe to him who dishonestly makes wealth for his house to place his nest on high, to escape from the reach of disaster!"

GIVING IN TO GUILT

Rather than succumbing to guilt, give to it. Give to your source of inspiration a tenth of the profit on each stream of income—this is all that is required; no guilt should be felt for retaining and using the remaining ninety percent.

The history of giving a tenth (tithing) is much broader than simply the biblical context. Throughout history, even in early Babylonia, tithing was customary. (Ponder, 1962)

For those of the Judeo-Christian tradition, tithing plays a notable role in bringing about the massive blessings received by Abraham, Isaac, and Jacob (Genesis 28:10-22). The Old Testament wraps up with God chastising his people for stealing from Him by not tithing and promising to unleash His bounty on them if they do resume tithing. (Malachi 3:7-2)

Joyfully giving to God in order to receive an even greater blessing is not bribery; it's being faithful in the little things so that as the increase comes, we return even more to God. He wants more income to benefit His church, and the way for Him to receive more is by sending favor to those who demonstrate they will give a portion to Him.

Regardless of your spiritual beliefs, giving provides other tangible benefits to release abundance in your life. Whether you recognize it or not. First, it helps erase any guilt you might feel regarding what you have. Second, giving provides deep subconscious signals to your mind, that you have enough abundance to share and you know how to receive more.

> *Joyful giving releases the abundance around you in ways duty-filled grudging giving cannot.*
> —**Paul Huber** *Killing Complacency*

CHAPTER NINE

THE DEATH OF COMPLACENCY – PART 2

While a fixed mindset, envy, and guilt place a cap on believing how much we can and should grow and achieve, complacent comfort and sedation cause us to not care to seek more.

When we lack the discomfort associated with scarcity, we lose the power of broke. When we soothe the discomfort, we sedate ourselves with substances (legal or not) and our imagination.

KILLING COMPLACENT COMFORT

> *To succeed, get comfortable being uncomfortable.*
> —**Paul Huber** *Killing Complacency*

For many, the source of complacency is comfort—or minimal discomfort—in their current situation. When the discomfort of being broke is high enough, some people channel it to drive themselves out of discomfort into a place of comfort or even great success. In his

books, "Shark Tank" star and FUBU founder Daymond John explored how he channeled *The Power of Broke* to drive himself to *Rise and Grind.* (John, 2016) (John, 2018) While some of the wealthy drive themselves to unhealthy, unbalanced lives due to the fear of returning to broke, many more people fail to rise to the level of their potential, because they are comfortable enough where they are.

When the discomfort of the situation is not high enough, even those with a growth mindset can become stuck. Instead of feeling the power of broke, we become complacent because of our comfort. Instead of fearing getting left behind by a changing world, we fear (or dislike) the pain and discomfort associated with growth. There is no staying the same, though—there is only advancing or retreating.

The things that grow us are *not* inherently pleasurable, though we may enjoy the resulting growth. Using deliberate practice as the route to mastery is not even enjoyed by those who achieve world-class levels of near perfection. The masters report deliberate practice as unpleasant, but enjoy the results much more than they dislike the pain of practice.

Repeated post-workout pain for Arnold Schwarzenegger was certainly not pleasant as he spent a decade building his body to win Mr. Universe six times. However, it was pleasant for me as Arnold recalled this experience during his one season hosting "The Celebrity Apprentice." During one episode, as the women's team started their second consecutive time in the boardroom, Snooki admitted to being "uncomfortable," saying who should be terminated. Arnold told Snooki that, while training for the world championship in bodybuilding, if he had trained only to his comfort level and then stopped, he wouldn't have won.

I am amazed by how often preachers are comfortable quoting James 1:5 (HCSB) without context, "Now if any of you lacks wisdom, he should ask God, who gives to all generously and without criticizing, and it will be given to him." The context, though, shows James understood growth comes through pain and trials, "Consider it a great joy, my brothers, whenever you experience various trials, knowing that the testing of your faith produces endurance. But endurance must do its complete work, so that you may be mature and complete, lacking nothing." (James 1:2-4, HCSB)

Finding wisdom only through your own trials is especially painful. While some education in the school of hard knocks is unavoidable, the more expedient route is through formal and informal education. From textbooks to biographies to the Bible, if we are humble enough to learn from other's hard knocks, we can accelerate our learning. But like bodybuilding, it does take reps: read, take notes, apply, evaluate, adjust, apply, read, take notes, apply, evaluate, adjust, apply, read…

If we are unwilling to take charge of our own growth—becoming comfortable being uncomfortable—nobody else will. Our boss, friends, or family may try to provide some motivation, but the ultimate factor is internal. Failure to learn and grow may one day lead to external motivators as we are forced to find a new job, friend, or spouse. We may receive some other swift kick in the rear as either a natural consequence of our negligence or as a divine motivational strategy. Ultimately, it's an individual's responsibility to either be proactive or to respond in the right way to a setback.

KILLING SEDATION

With our dreams dead, bleak prospects of growth, and feelings of envy and/or guilt, it's easy to turn to what Garrett White calls sedation. (White, 2017) Rather than fixing our problems, we turn to television. Instead of filling our lives with activities that bring us energy, we sedate with another round of Candy Crush. Instead of filling our lives with the meaning our soul craves, we seek the pleasure of sex, which was not designed to last. Instead of seeing our reality as it is and working to change it, we medicate our way out of our pain with food, drugs, or alcohol ... I'm bored, just one more brownie... it's 5:00 somewhere... is it 4:20 yet?

Beyond medicating with substances and mindless entertainment, it's easy to imagine our success rather than seeking it. Porn allows people to imagine and see the pleasure of sex without all of the patience and work of a relationship, and the random hookup is nothing more than two-player porn. But fulfilling our animal desires for sex is only the start. Vicariously living out success through television and social media serves the same role for success in our lives. While it can serve as inspiration and entertainment, too often, it serves to replace success instead of inspiring it.

Regardless of whether the sedation is sinful, illegal, or not inherently wrong, sedation saps our energy and pulls us away from our purpose in life. Whether we are comfortably complacent or wallowing in our own misery, sedation traps us in our current state through inaction, counterproductive action, or wasted action.

There is certainly a time for rest, recovery, and procreation; and discerning the difference between sedation and relaxation is another instance of discernment we need to practice.

> *"I have the right to do anything,"*
> *you say—but not everything is*
> *beneficial. "I have the right to do*
> *anything"—but not everything is*
> *constructive.*
> *—1 Corinthians 10:23 (NIV)*

The Apostle Paul understood, regardless of whether something was right or wrong, that it may or may not be constructive or beneficial. When we kill sedation, we kill the drive for counterproductive and unproductive activities.

Without sedation in our lives, we have ample energy to focus on the core four areas of life: body, being, balance, and business. Nobody can muster the strength to go all out in one area of life for all of their waking hours. Arnold Schwarzenegger often worked out in two four-hour chunks, allowing his body to recover as he built his mind with business classes and worked at his day job.

We all make work-life choices as we prioritize how much time we spend on the job or on the rest of our lives. (Welch, 2009) The choice to build his body meant Arnold had less time for other areas of his life. By choosing to be proactive rather than sedating ourselves, we have more time and energy to learn, grow, and advance, without sacrificing other areas of our lives. By making prudent prioritization of our time, we determine how fit we are in each area of our lives.

CHAPTER TEN

THE PASSION AND PURPOSE DRIVING YOUR LIFE

For decades we have been told to follow our passions or to ignore our passions; our purpose is all about ourselves or all about God, and everyone other than ourselves. It's little wonder why everyone is confused.

Without passion, work is just a grind; and without purpose, life is just a biological event. With some rare exceptions, our purpose is not announced before our birth or trumpeted from heaven. Instead, our passions evolve as we experience life, and our purpose and calling revealed incrementally.

Much of how we view our work is based on the mindset we have toward it. A key illustration comes from the old parable of the bricklayers as retold in *Grit*:

> *Three bricklayers are asked: "What are you doing?" The first says, "I am laying bricks." The second says, "I am building a church." And the third says, "I am building the house of God."*

 COMPLACENCY

Ultimately, as long as your work is not illegal or something you find immoral, it should be celebrated as your contribution to society. If someone is willing to pay for it, your work is something valued by the employer / consumer and society. The amount of the paycheck is not an indication of the value of a person, rather an indication of how rare and valuable their skills are.

> *Your value as a person, and the value of your labor are two different things. Confusing one for the other is demoralizing and demotivating.*
> —**Paul Huber** *Killing Complacency*

THE PASSION MYTH

Steve Jobs famously told 2005 Stanford graduates (and the world) to follow their passions. However, the history of his own life reveals he did much the opposite. In college, he studied history and dance, while also experimenting with eastern religions—passion alone could have made him a dancing monk. However, when he tired of being broke, he applied his marketing prowess to complement Steve Wozniack's engineering intellect in the creation of Apple Computers. (Newport, 2012)

It's not that passion is bad—it isn't. Instead, the problems are supply, demand, and lack of experience.

By the time a student finishes high school, typical self-reported passions include music, sports, and art—where there is high supply and low demand, resulting in low salaries for all but those at the very top of their fields, where salaries explode to envious levels—more on that later.

Further, passion is not necessarily something instilled when we are young—especially as we prepare to select a college major. Instead, passion arises from doing and experiencing. Through broad experiences, people are able to find which areas excite them and which fail to. Ultimately, finding passion comes through persistence in an area that was initially unenticing. Passion is the result, rather than the source of our efforts. (Duckworth, 2016)

Celebrities and others in high profile, passion-centric professions like to promote following your passion the way they did. However, those who achieve success away from the limelight typically arrive at their passion through building proficiency in the mundane and the ordinary. Passion follows more often than it leads.

Understanding the dynamics of a small family owned business, and believing the passion myth (at the time) and, frankly, being a bit of a jerk, I once asked a second-generation jewelry store owner where he got his passion for jewelry. I doubt my son's homeschool classmates grasped how amazing his response was—he became passionate about gems toward the end of his gemology studies at college.

This son dutifully followed his father into the jewelry business and spent years at school for something where he initially lacked passion. Instead of becoming resentful, he found passion by becoming proficient—through mastery he found passion. In the same way, Grant Cardone hated selling and the car business. However, by replacing his loathing with learning and his whining with winning, Grant was able to become one of the best car salesmen in the business. By learning to love what others found repulsive, Grant scaled beyond the earning power available to him at a single dealership, and began training sales professionals across the country and throughout the world. Because his programs provide immense value to so many, he is able to earn substantial income and employ numerous people.

THE MOTIVATION MYTH

Just as passion is the effect rather than the cause, motivation—real intrinsic motivation, and not the drive to avoid pain—is the result of action, rather than the spark igniting action. (Haden, 2018) This, perhaps, is why arts and sports can be so easily motivational. At the beginning of training, a little learning, practice, and feedback results in basic ability and the motivating feedback of demonstrable improvement.

The early stages—even the first 20 hours—of deliberate practice can move a newbie to a presentable level of skill. (Kaufman, 2013) For many of us, adding a new tool to our toolbox of skills is well worth the investment of 20 hours, even if we are at or just above the beginner level.

After the initial phase of improvement, though, it becomes harder and harder to make improvements, and motivation can wane, as described in *The Dip*. (Godin, 2007) Ultimately, it's those who have the persistence to last through *The Dip*, being motivated by the end goal or the minuscule improvements coming after an initial level of competence, who achieve world-class mastery. Again, it's discernment, like that described in *The Dip*, which enables an individual to determine when to drive toward achieving world-class mastery, and when they are good enough at a skill to improve their work, relationships, or enjoyment of life.

THE TRUTH ABOUT YOUR PURPOSE

Your purpose should neither be taken lightly nor lead to paralysis by analysis—and it's typically not revealed all at once lest it scares or underwhelms you. The best option is to take it day-by-day and year-by-year—not foregoing the hard grind of the day-to-day or periodic reflection.

We all have a deeply embedded drive to find meaning and purpose in our lives, as Victor Frankl explored in *Man's Search for Meaning*. (Frankl, 1959) Perhaps explaining why the passion myth resonates so deeply. It's easy to think purpose only comes through achieving what elevates us to celebrity status, instead

of the daily obedience of getting our job done, sharpening our skills, and pressing on to the next goal.

Arnold was not hatched as the Governator. He ground through his daily workouts, sharpened his bodybuilding and business acumen, and eventually achieved his first big goal of winning Mr. Universe. It took more years of hard work—sustaining his current job while preparing for the next one—before he was able to become an actor, building his skills and value incrementally, until he eventually achieved superstar status, all the while working on business deals outside of the public's view.

Through hard work and deliberate planning, he eventually became governor of California. Imagine if, as a boy in Austria, Schwarzenegger had learned he would one day become governor... he may have quit before he started or relaxed and waited for his destiny to find him.

PURPOSE IN THE PATH

Arnold's progression from scrawny Austrian lad to Governor of California provides one example of moving from purpose to purpose—major goal to major goal. The same way King David, of David and Goliath fame, moved from one God-ordained assignment to the next. Both men represent that even though the purpose of their lives includes a prestigious role, the path to their ultimate role includes significant contributions along the way.

The path itself provides purpose—both in shaping the person for the pinnacle of their purpose, and by providing value to the world around them.

NO CALLING IS HIGHER THAN OTHERS

It's easy to believe that people living out their calling by working in a charitable organization have a higher calling—especially when many of them tell us they do. We see this whether they feel called to save the whales or save souls. However, there is no higher or lower calling, only following *your* calling or not.

We have both general, universal callings and individual, specific callings. (Bevere, 2017) People of faith are called to live a life furthering God's kingdom—all are called to be good people and to care for our world. AND we are called to make the most of what we have been given—our ambitions, the skills we have developed, and the innate capacity we possess. Weighting one too heavily or lightly skews our perspective.

For most of us, our most notable specific calling is our work. Not to say the rest of life is unimportant, but our work is where we spend most of our time, energy, and waking hours. Whether our work is in an office, factory, or the home, we are called to work. Our current job may help us survive on our path to the next step in our calling, or it may be the pinnacle of our calling. Whether our work is like being the lead actor, a supporting actor, or cast and crew, living out our calling through our work is spiritually significant.

> *Work is integral in how we execute our calling. Work is not some unspiritual activity we redeem through tithing, sharing the gospel with our coworkers, and volunteering during the off hours. Work often* **is** *the calling, and then we do the other things too.*
> —**Paul Huber** *Killing Complacency*

Your purpose is two-fold. First, to fulfill your unique personal calling through your work is critical for sustaining our society. Second, to fulfill the general calling of loving God and loving the people around you—your neighbors. Both are important—one calls out who you are, the other calls out whose you are.

Though our work is an expression of our calling, one specific job or type of job is not. Even if one role, one job, one path to purpose is blocked, choose to find an alternate route.

MEMBERS OF THE SAME BODY

Whether in society in general or the church, we are all members of one body (1 Corinthians 12:12-31). Each of us has our own calling and our own role to play—both in our current truth and the future reality we are trying to build. Whether by nature, nurture, or divine positioning, we have a certain personality and skill set. Contentment will lead a person to not desire to be something they cannot be; overcoming complacency means they will work to be the best version of themselves.

Because those called to be the mouth gain our attention, we may look at them with envy as the spotlight turns to them, or be bothered by the means employed to carry out their calling. And because we are wired to dislike the pain of accountability, we may deride those who seek to hold us accountable, referring to them as being at the other end of the digestive tract. However, both callings are critical to spreading the word and to maintaining hygiene.

There are no wrong callings—only wrong ways to execute the callings.

Strength in the proverbial body means we are all working to be very best at what we are called to do, and not envying those with other callings. However, our calling for today may be different than our calling for tomorrow. Our path to our final calling typically has waypoints along the path, where we must first be faithful with the little before we are entrusted with the greater calling. Discerning contentment from complacency is critical in knowing when to persevere and when to pivot.

DON'T QUIT YOUR DAY JOB

Frequently, a new believer has a burning passion for their newfound belief. However, as the Apostle Paul

advised in 1 Corinthians 7:17-24, they should not just drop out of their day job. As discussed above, your job is an integral part of your calling, which likely stays the same before and after salvation.

John Bevere's *Called* provides three examples of this: (Bevere, 2017)

1. **A Navy SEAL:** who initially thought he was called to be a pastor but instead determined he was called to be a SEAL.

2. **Professional Golfer:** who thought he should spend more time sharing his faith, and as a result, let his golf game slip. By focusing more on his game, he was able to become more successful *and then* to become more influential than he otherwise would have been.

3. **John himself:** started as an engineer but eventually figured out he was called to ministry.

By listening for their calling, each person was able to figure out where to go—which often was not in the ministry. The world needs maybe 1% paid clergy and 99% spreading the gospel through their actions, relationships, and giving.

The same holds true for those who want to improve other aspects of the world—stay focused on your primary calling rather than diminishing your impact by getting off track.

CHAPTER ELEVEN

GROWING WHERE YOU ARE

In my corner of Iowa, there are two competing bumper stickers shaped like the state. Inside one, the word "native" proclaims the lifelong residency of the driver. Inside the other, "captive" proclaims the driver would rather be somewhere else but is stuck here. While I can't claim native status, and I would rather live somewhere warmer, proclaiming the captive status cedes too much power outside of me. I am here because the discomfort is not too high, and the effort is too high to find and capture available options to work elsewhere.

TRAPPED

Life has a way of trapping us with responsibility. The American dream to buy a house lands most of us with 30 years of paying a mortgage, and high transaction costs whenever we want to move—slowing our ability to grab opportunities. The cars and consumer goods we want land us with even more recurring payments. Even if we don't have the responsibility of caring for our

offspring, it's easy to burden ourselves with monthly expenses we can't or don't want to eliminate.

Deferring, limiting, or eliminating these responsibilities clears the way for easier exploration and freedom of movement. However, it may already be too late, or assuming the responsibility might be the right thing to do. After all, who doesn't enjoy making babies? Most of us do want to raise the next generation.

The key is not to shirk responsibility. Instead, work within what you have. Use your current job to prepare for and fund the path to your next endeavor.

Daymond John continued to work at Red Lobster during the first few years of building FUBU. The job funded his living expenses as he worked to build the clothing company. (John, 2016)

My day job not only funds my lifestyle and provides financial resources to work on my side hustles, but it also provides opportunities to improve my writing and communication skills through the course of my work. Sure, it focuses more on explaining complex technical information, and persuading potential buyers to choose our products, but the corollaries between the two allow my job to improve my side hustle, and my side hustle to improve my work. For example, all of the writing during off-hours has allowed my work documents to be even more clear and reader-friendly.

BUILD TRANSFERABLE SKILLS

No matter where you are, you can build skills that are useful elsewhere. Being able to communicate effectively through both written and spoken means is incredibly important. Warren Buffett, one of the richest people in the world, credits much of his success to being able to speak effectively. Not just to avoid having his knees knock while speaking, but being able to speak even though his knees were knocking. Rather than avoiding opportunities to present, like so many of my peers want to do, seize them as opportunities to hone this important skill.

Programs like Toastmasters have centered around not only providing time to speak, but also evaluation times which allow the speaker to gain valuable feedback to make future presentations even better. In addition to improving the speaking itself, evaluations are important practice in both giving and receiving feedback.

Other opportunities for building transferrable skills are highly dependent on your current and desired field. In the case of Adam Corolla, as he prepared for his eventual comedic fame, he turned his boring job teaching court-mandated driver's education, into instruction providing the required information with all the flair of his stand-up routines. Corolla also endured volunteer and underpaid work as he built his comedy skills to the level he could use them to make a living. (Corolla, 2012)

Did you notice it was more than just paid work that can build transferrable skills? Often our hobbies and volunteer work provide the right platform for building skills that transfer to our next stop. Side hustles, volunteering, and hobbies all provide opportunities to gain skills with low risk. In the process of gaining useful skills, we may make or lose a little money, or feel good about how we spend our time, and gain the benefit of building our value.

Volunteering pays dividends not just in the karmic sense; put good into the universe, and get good back out through the positive feelings produced. Volunteering pays dividends through building skills, relationships, and confidence where the stakes are much lower than at your day job.

GROW DEEPER

The grass is greenest where you water it—and where the dog does her business. The moral of the saying is not to make a mess where you are, but to fertilize and water where you are. The last chapter inverted the passion and motivation myths—they come as the result of doing, rather than as the inspiration for doing. Growing deeper where you are, if it's a suitable area, can be the best answer to flagging motivation and feelings of lack of purpose.

Early in his life, after the death of his father, Grant Cardone became obsessed with the sedation of sex, drugs, and alcohol. The obsession nearly cost him his life. Rather than giving up all obsessions, Grant shifted to healthy obsessions. He became obsessed with his job of selling cars—so obsessed he eventually shifted his career to selling sales training classes. By growing deeper, Cardone moved from hating his job to being good enough to train masses of people in the sales process. (Cardone, 2016)

In growing deeper, Grant had to demonstrate an exceptional depth of knowledge in the domain (or field) of cars. He had to know not only his own product, but also the products of his competitors. In parallel, he had to build a depth of knowledge in his discipline—selling. The ability to sell effectively transcends the specific product being sold.

In my field of engineering, I advocate the same building of depth in both the domain and the discipline. But I take it a few steps further…

BECOME Y-SHAPED

Back in 1999, Ideo gained recognition on Nightline for their innovative methods of innovation. At the time, they were already one of the most influential design companies in the world. The teams are eclectic—focused on applying their process for innovation.

Since then, CEO Tim Brown has said he wants to work with T-shaped people—referring to their experience, not their physique. He seeks employees who have depth in one domain or discipline, and broad interests in areas which aren't core to their business—usually expressed in the form of unusual hobbies and non-work endeavors.

The theory is that depth is needed to really understand one targeted domain or another, and breadth is what brings innovation to the problem they have been hired to solve.

As I work with engineers to develop large and complex embedded computing systems, I see the need for more than just a T-shaped shallow breadth and isolated depth. My visualization of the ideal engineer is much more Y-shaped—with big serifs, both in terms of experience and day-to-day behavior. Of course, the same Y-shaped concept can be applied to a multitude of job types.

The broad experience Tim Brown values is truly important, as represented by the big serifs in the Y-shaped experience model. Taking the analogy further, though, the best engineers have depth in both their domain (avionics display systems, communications, or navigation, as examples from my employer's domains) as well as in their chosen disciplines (e.g., software, electrical or mechanical engineering). This depth expands into assembling a rich mental model of the system they are developing. The mental model maps their piece into the larger whole, and allows them to make design decisions with more information providing context. The other arm of the Y represents the behavior of engineers as they collaborate with their peers on the other side of an interface, or cross-train to build bench strength or speed development of a function or feature.

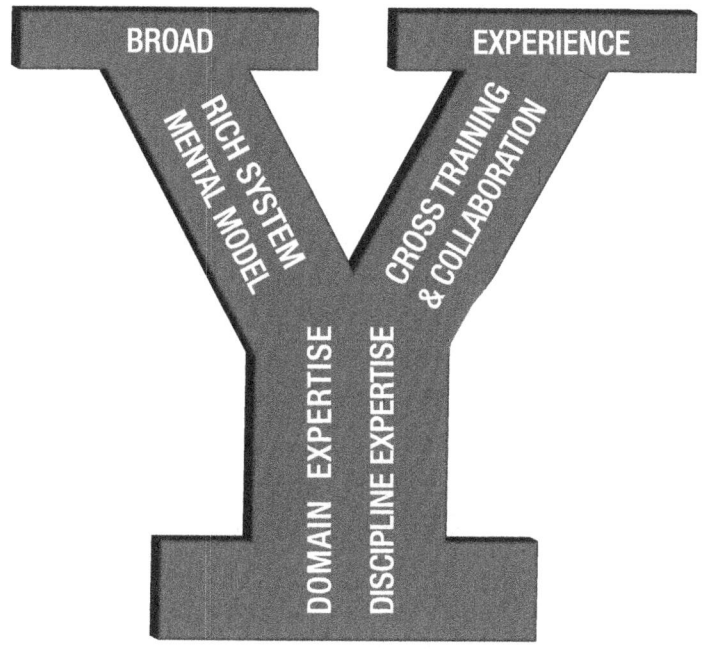

Extending the example of Grant Cardone's experience as a car salesman, he would have demonstrated being Y-shaped through:

- **Domain expertise** in the features and benefits of the cars he sold *and* those of his competitors.

- **Discipline expertise** in the process of selling and closing a deal.

- **Rich system metal model** so he understood how the dealership worked to make happy customers.

- **Cross-training and collaboration** so he understood what customers would go through in the finance and delivery process—after he completed his work.

- **Broad experience** in areas he could use to relate to the experience of customers.

CHASE ADJACENT AREAS

Most business leaders know the most prudent strategy is to pursue areas, which are adjacent to their current business. Rather than turning coal miners into software developers, they teach coal miners to mine for other materials, or use heavy equipment to build roads and bridges. Aerospace manufacturers build for both commercial and defense markets, and automakers provide a range of offerings from entry-level to luxury.

Though makers of horse-drawn carriages quickly dwindled with the introduction of the automobile, the prudent ones moved not to luxury carriages, but to build bodies and accessories for the new horse-less carriages.

Anyone currently in a dwindling industry should look in adjacent areas and prepare for a move. Anyone wanting a more fulfilling field should not look for a complete reset, but something related to the skills they already have.

When becoming Y-shaped, understanding adjacent work functions and adjacent activities at work can provide continuity without changing employers.

As computer systems were emerging in businesses, there was a slow transition from teletype systems to more modern forms like faxes and then emails. In my company, there was an expert teletype maintenance and repairman. He could have easily transitioned into the nascent information technology department, but instead of changing with technology, he doubled-down on being the best teletype expert. Eventually, we had to let him go because there was no work he was qualified to do.

THE BLUE OCEAN STRATEGY FOR PERSONAL SUCCESS

In addition to seeking adjacent opportunities, businesses often choose to move into areas where there is little to no competition. Aggressive cost-cutting and other competitive moves have made their portion of the ocean red, so they develop strategies to move into a blue part of the ocean—*The Blue Ocean Strategy.* (Kim & Maubourgne, 2014)

Applying this strategy to You Inc., consider moves leveraging your skills, interests, and education in ways, which move you into a blue ocean. Sometimes, it's a unique blend of skills that provide differentiation in an area of unexpected opportunity.

The performing arts are saturated with would-be celebrities and those who love their chosen art. Because of high supply and low demand for all but the top tier, wages are often minuscule—squeezing out anyone without a viable main job or patron. One young theater major gave up when facing the bleak odds of success. However, as she pursued a career in construction, she was able to fill a niche for performance facility construction. By combining her passion for and understanding of the stage with her day job of construction, she had the opportunity to spend every day on things that excite her.

BUILD A STRATEGY FOR YOU, INC.

As CEO of You Inc., it's your responsibility to build a corporate strategy. You are relying on you. Do you need to go deeper where you are? Do you need to move to a new area? Someplace adjacent or completely new? Can you ride your domain and disciplines into retirement, or do you need to refresh your abilities? As CEO, these are questions only you can answer.

Just like any CEO, you will benefit from a board of directors who can help advise you. The board should care about You Inc., but should not be invested to the point where they benefit from the direction you take. This is the definition of a disinterested third-party— not someone without interest, but someone without a stake in the results.

CHAPTER TWELVE

LEARN FROM THE SUCCESS OF OTHERS

The School of Hard Knocks charges oppressively high tuition. All too often, our own hubris leads us to rush into situations where others have already paid the price. Rather than having the humility to learn from our board of directors, books, and instructors, our ego leads us into ill-advised situations.

Ego leads us to think we know more than others. (In the big-head sense of the term, not the clinical psychology sense of ego.) Ego makes us think we are better than others—that we have something they don't—that we can succeed where they didn't. Ego makes us think we don't need to learn any more. Simply, *Ego is the Enemy.* (Holiday, 2016)

THE SUCCESS ALGORITHM

I spent a chunk of my career working on business process improvement, at the time when American companies were working on learning "Lean" from the Toyota Production System. In factories, we were using tools like Six Sigma to stamp out process variation, eliminate waste, and accelerate product delivery. All of these were worthy goals and necessary to stay competitive in an ever-changing and improving environment.

However, too many American companies only received half of the lessons from Toyota – and, with the Lean moniker, only viewed the process as the elimination of waste rather than improving the process of adding value. Desiring only the shorter-term benefits of cost savings, rather than the long-term benefits of a value increasing culture. Seeking to mass-produce "best practices" rather than seeking to build a learning machine, which produces tremendous value and builds great practices from first principles rather than by replicating what others have done.

To the typical "Lean" practitioner, Toyota engages in counter-intuitive behaviors that seem not to have the Lean behaviors they would expect. From assigning process improvement students a three-foot circle from which to observe a process for a full day, to flying teams from one factory to another to learn how the other works, Toyota invests heavily in improving people and not just processes. (Liker, 2004)

Rather than cookie-cutter replication of process improvements between factories, the people of Toyota learn from what is working and seek to apply the principles to each unique situation as it's presented.

Andy Grove, co-founder and long-serving leader of computer chip maker Intel, demonstrated learning from analogies and principles rather than best practice replication. As Grove was discussing his challenges with Clayton Christiansen, author of *The Innovator's Dilemma,* Christiansen taught Grove and his team *how to think* rather than teaching them *what to think.*

Rather than guiding them to a single great innovation, Christiansen taught them about the process of disruptive innovation. (Christensen, 1997) The lesson learned was not simply how to develop the next new product, but how to ensure the company continually developed one new disruptive product after the next—disrupting themselves rather than waiting for the competition to do so. Of course, like any organization, Intel still has blind spots, and they were largely shutout of the tablet and smartphone computing market.

SUCCESS POISON

In addition to the absence of a formula for success, there are countless ways to poison the path to success. Failing to kill complacency induced by envy and coveting, poisons our opportunities for success. Is that source of complacency really dead in your life, or was that just attempted murder? It can be an ongoing effort to overcome jealousy—one that must be consciously renewed by remembering to be excited for the success of others rather than envious of it.

Once envy is sufficiently suppressed, you have the opportunity to open your mind to learning from the success of others. Though envy may never be completely gone, keeping it out of the forefront of our minds allows us to be honestly inquisitive about how others reached their success—truly learning from it rather than allowing ourselves to be bothered by it.

Furthermore, eliminating the cognitive dissonance caused by envy allows us to believe success is a worthy outcome based on the hard work we endure.

PLAYING THE ODDS

The life and experiences of Wild West celebrity James Butler "Wild Bill" Hickock provide an excellent thought experiment for illustrating how success is about playing the odds:

We meet Wild Bill at the Gem Theater. Which is not so much a real theater, but a bar and brothel where the "upstairs girls" entertain bar patrons between customers seeking the world's oldest profession. Though the heat of the day faded quickly outside, the place is still hot from the crowd inside, and the smell of the horses in the streets is wafting in. Wild Bill is enjoying the wild west version of the pink drink—a gin and bitters.

> **Whippersnapper:** "Wild Bill, tell me about how I can have the same sort of amazing success you have had." [without getting assassinated]

> **Wild Bill:** "As a successful poker player, the first thing I had to learn was how to play the odds associated with the winning and losing hands. I know the winning hands are rare, and the losing hands are common, but I leave it up to the accountants to know the exact ratios of

each. But knowing the odds is just the beginning—I have also learned to observe the others at the table."

Whippersnapper: "What do you think about all of the men out here in Deadwood prospecting?"

Wild Bill: "Most of them are fools. My accountant friend tells me the odds of getting a royal flush are worse than one in half a million. Most of the prospectors are playing with about the same odds of making it big, but they don't have the support they need in order to play a game with such poor odds. What's worse is as soon as most of them get any money, it's spent on booze or whores."

Whippersnapper: "So, what I hear you saying is that the business to be in is providing the booze and the whores."

Wild Bill: "I won't deny a lot of money flows that way. Look at the owner here, Al Swerengen. He profits when the men are down, wanting a drink and some companionship, and he profits when they feel the need to celebrate in the same way. However, he is catering to the base desires of the men around here; and he keeps the girls in line with violence and threats of violence. And he is often forced to deal with the violence of his customers."

Whippersnapper: "I know you have enjoyed the kinds of products Al has provided, so what do you think is better than running a place like this?"

Wild Bill: "I know I really ought to avoid the goods here, but let me tell you who really has it figured out. Seth Bullock, the sheriff of Deadwood, is also one of the leading businessmen here—it's like money is rolling downhill to him."

Bullock: "Now wait a minute; it's not like people are just giving me money for fun. My business partner and I invested a lot of money in inventory and then risked traveling through the frontier to get here. In exchange for my inventory, people give me money. Sure, it's more than I paid, but the profit covers additional expenses, including the occasional losses we suffer as the resupply travels to get here. We are currently expanding our investments by bringing in the equipment needed to build a brick factory. In addition to supplying bricks which are not flammable like the wood construction we have now, we will also provide jobs for the men who build the bricks."

Wild Bill: "I wasn't saying you are lucky, just that you know how to play the odds the right way. The odds of success in prospecting are very hit and miss. The job of bar and brothel owner is morally suspect. But your job as businessman provides value here, and in turn, you receive a portion of the value to enjoy life and a portion to reinvest in your business. Even if I don't like all of the terms of your deals, the community benefits by having the products we need."

Whippersnapper: "Now I understand. I should be a part of something where I can feel good about what I am doing, and I should start a business that gives me good odds of success."

Wild Bill: "Right, but you don't have to be the business owner, and you don't have to go it alone. I have my partner Charlie Utter; Bullock has a business partner too. And there are a lot of good men and women working for them— being a part of someone else's endeavor can be rewarding too."

[Inspiration for the above was provided by the dramatized history of Deadwood in the book *Deadwood*. (Dexter, 1986)]

What are you doing to improve the odds of your success? Can you live with the kind of success you seek?

> *Success is less about winning some kind of lottery and more about choosing a trajectory toward success — playing the odds of beneficial learning and endeavors.*
> —**Paul Huber** *Killing Complacency*

CASE STUDIES

Discussing case studies is the backbone of business schools. At You Inc., well-written biographies, auto-biographies, and historical accounts can be valuable sources of case studies. In the "Painful Prologue" to *Ego is the Enemy,* Ryan Holiday provides a well-written account of not just what he did right to rise in his field, but the painful mistakes he made along the way. To be useful as a case study, and well written, the account must include the failures and lessons learned along the way, rather than just the successes experienced. (Holiday, 2016)

We are wired to expect a clean narrative describing the causes of success and a clean progression to a desirable outcome—but reality is not neat and tidy like that.

Here are some great case studies which I have enjoyed to kick-start your search for instructive books:

Can't Hurt Me is David Goggins's account of descending into self-loathing misery and rise into having the mental toughness to become a Navy SEAL and ultra-marathon runner. (Goggins, 2018)

American Icon describes the errors Ford Motor Company made to get into serious trouble and the work Alan Mulally did to get them out of it. Yes, it focuses on the successful aspects of Mulally's work, but it also investigates the failings that provided the opportunity for him. (Hoffman, 2013)

Ego is the Enemy starts with Ryan Holiday's personal case study and then provides a series of historical studies. (Holiday, 2016)

Shut Up and Listen! recounts Tilman Fertitta's rise in the hospitality industry and the paddles that were looking for his backside along the way. (Fertitta & Gray, 2019)

Beginner's Pluck describes the process of beginning a for-profit business that also helps young African women receive a college education. (Bohannon, 2019)

Crushing: God Turns Pressure into Power includes both the wilderness years T. D. Jakes experienced on the path to becoming a recognized pastor, and the crushing he experienced after notoriety arrived. (Jakes, 2019)

Find your own case studies from people and events that inspire you while remembering the process probably was not as simple and straightforward as described.

> *Success leaves clues.*
> — *Tony Robbins*

SPECIAL BONUS OFFER
GO TO

pauljhuber.com/kc-bonuses
to download exclusive
content for readers of
Killing Complacency.

CHAPTER THIRTEEN

DO YOU DESERVE WHAT YOU WANT?

It's human nature to desire abundance. However, it's also in our animal nature to conserve our energy by avoiding the exertion of working. The cheetah demonstrates this dichotomy by spending most of its time lounging around like a giant house cat, and mere moments at its famously blistering speed.

Because there is a correlation between how hard we work and the resulting rewards, most of us are only motivated to work enough to attain the lifestyle we deem adequate, rather than the abundant lifestyle. In fact, it's easy to desire rewards without work. However, as Warren Buffett's business partner observes:

> *To get what you want, you have to deserve what you want. The world is not yet a crazy enough place to reward a whole bunch of unde-serving people.*
> *—Charles T. Munger*

Similarly, complacency can build as we grind away at the exhausting tedium of our day-to-day jobs, without planning the strategy needed to become deserving of more.

RESPONSIBLE FOR RESULTS

Truly deserving something—having earned the expected outcome tends to NOT align with our modern usage of the word. We say we deserve a good job, a healthy relationship, a worthy partner... but have we earned it? Have we sought relationships with healthy people?

Deserving, in the sense Munger uses the word and the way it's used in this book, means we have done what we ought to—probably more than we feel we needed to—in order to earn the outcome. When we allow our ego to dictate what we deserve, it's easy to feel entitled to a result long before we have done the hard work to earn it.

To mitigate the plague of unduly feeling entitled, Dr. John Townsend recommends shifting your language—especially your thoughts—from phrases that include words like "deserve" and "entitled", to the word "responsible." Though the shift may seem subtle, the impact is clear. Just like defeating the enemy of the ego, becoming responsible for outcomes shifts the mindset. (Townsend, 2015)

I am responsible for becoming qualified for the job I desire. I am responsible for a healthy relationship with my partner—or finding someone with whom I can have a healthy relationship. I am responsible for maintaining a size that allows me to continue to fit into my car.

> *Taking responsibility for results moves us from a passive, victim mindset to an action-focused mindset.*
> —**Paul Huber** *Killing Complacency*

WORKING TO BE DESERVING

Working hard though, is just one part of deserving what you want. The hard work must drive in the direction of providing value now, and building your own future value. Moreover, wisdom and luck play a part in the effectiveness of the work and the value of the path.

I often see some of my fellow engineers desire an equation or process for everything we are doing—including driving for success. However, there is no equation for success. Instead, life is full of numerous probabilistic activities that lead to or away from success. If you adjust based on the feedback provided by failures, you can do as John Maxwell says: *Sometimes You Win—Sometimes You Learn.* (Maxwell J. C., 2015)

Perhaps the most cited probabilistic success relationship is the correlation between having a college degree and increased income in adulthood. On average, college graduates earn more than those with just a high school diploma—and without completing high school, job prospects are even worse. Further study reveals some degrees lead to higher-paying jobs which relate to the field of study, while other degrees provide little to no real return on investment—leading to careers which are no better than what a high school diploma provides.

Understanding the odds of a positive return on investments like four (or more) years of college is just one way to bring discernment to important decisions. When choosing between various interesting options, the next layer of wisdom is to look at long-term trends and to select based on the best long-term prospect.

Of course, even the most well thought out decisions can result in a dead-end, diminishing results, or a nagging feeling to change trajectory after investing decades into a career. Discernment is knowing when the time is right to continue and when to pivot. There is a time to continue pushing through until results are seen—proficiency leads to pleasure, or the world catches up to your brilliance. There is also a time to recognize folly, make a course correction, or to prepare for a new season.

Entrepreneurs are sometimes defined as, "someone who risks time and/or money in exchange for the chance at a financial reward." While employees risk someone else's money, entrepreneurs risk their own time and money—just like investing in the prospects of building your own personal value.

Since you are the CEO of the one-person, entrepreneurial company that is your life, You Inc., you have similar responsibilities to any other CEO.

> *As the CEO of your life, it's your responsibility to manage the risks associated with the investment of your time, effort, and money. The return may be financial or intangible, but it must be worth the investment and risk.*
> —**Paul Huber** *Killing Complacency*

The promotion of college as a low-risk investment of years of life and thousands of dollars, coupled with low-cost student loans has driven up demand, resulting in ever-increasing costs. Further, public support of higher education has often resulted in poor financial stewardship, keeping both the total cost of education and the cost to the students at an elevated level. These increased costs mean there is a diminishing return on the invested time and money.

Alternatives to higher education continue to expand as opportunities grow in e-commerce, the service industries, and other places require training but not the high costs of a four-year degree.

While formal post-secondary education is regulated with thorough accreditation standards, the alternative sources of learning are not. The result is consumers must be more diligent in ensuring not only is the program worth the investment, but also the work of executing the resulting strategy is worth the additional investment required.

RISKY PROPOSITIONS

Not all of the probabilistic propositions are investments with potential rewards. Often, people seek pleasure with the hope there is no negative consequence that results, or there is an easy recovery from it.

Sex is a great illustration here. It exists to ensure the continuance of the species, and it's pleasurable and desirable to help ensure the population is growing rather than shrinking. Like investments, it's a probabilistic scenario. The odds of pleasure are near 100%, but the odds of other outcomes, like disease or pregnancy, have a variety of factors and potential end results.

Following biblical guidelines for sex not only eliminates the spread of sexually transmitted diseases, but it also ensures that if pregnancy results (whether planned on not), the child will enter a relatively stable home.

Further, people who complete high school, higher education, and get married before having children, are more likely to be financially successful, and are better able to provide for their families. Becoming a parent too soon usually prevents creating enough margin for making investments in increasing the value of their skills.

Regardless of how anybody feels about the morality of the situation, gluttony, drugs, sex, and drunkenness all offer short-term pleasures in exchange for the risk of undesirable consequences.

PERMISSIBLE, BUT NOT BENEFICIAL

In our world of great abundance (especially in the United States), we have significant amounts of time, effort, and money to channel to pursuits, that are neither morally debatable nor investments in our own futures. Some of these pursuits offer welcome rejuvenation from the daily grind. However, all too often, we waste away hours with a Netflix binge or in pursuit of achieving the next level in a game, which has no bearing on our lives or our family's.

The mental and physical benefits of rest are clear. However, if the results in your life are not at the desired level, it would be wise to take a look at how your discretionary time, effort, and money are being spent.

Beyond wise investment of time, too many of us sedate ourselves with being constantly busy or entertained. Without time to reflect, think, or feel, we avoid facing the demons of feeling inadequate or regretful. Rather than pursuing risky destructive behaviors, or working through the significant time and effort required to fix or address our feelings, we sedate ourselves with that which is permissible but not beneficial.

AN ABUNDANT MINDSET RETURNS ABUNDANCE

Good stewardship is not an exercise in miserliness—it's an exercise in finding the right, affordable next step. An abundant mindset is not simply expanding with the expectation of growth.

> *An abundance mindset recognizes that the only way to receive value is to provide value—making the largest responsible investment provides the largest opportunity for a return.*
> —**Paul Huber** *Killing Complacency*

Our bias to want a deal is very strong, and advertisers exploit it to the benefit of those hoping to sell us something. Too often, we hope something we acquire for little or no cost will provide the value we seek. Instead, we get what we paid for—which was not much.

If instead, we look for the very best our budget can responsibly afford, we will invest in the people, products, education, and services which best position us for the growth we need, and the success which is our responsibility—and not acquire toys distracting us from our mission.

For my fellow Christians who have had their stewardship metastasize into miserliness, consider this passage from Proverbs 11:24-26 (NIV):

> *One person gives freely, yet gains even more; another withholds unduly, but comes to poverty.*
>
> *A generous person will prosper; whoever refreshes others will be refreshed.*
>
> *People curse the one who hoards grain, but they pray God's blessing on the one who is willing to sell. (NIV)*

And this from 1 Timothy 5:18:

> *For Scripture says, "Do not muzzle an ox while it's treading out the grain," and "The worker deserves his wages."* (NIV)

If instead of taking responsible steps toward growth, we hoard our time and money, the result will be contraction and poverty. If we seek to have something beneficial, paying a fair price to its provider gives us the best chance at reaping the desired gains.

THERE IS NOT ONE WHO IS WORTHY

Deserving our success is nothing like deserving entry into heaven. Deserving our success is the result of focused effort in a beneficial direction—and slipping up once in a while is a normal result of taking some risks.

If we wanted to deserve entry into heaven, we would have to be perfect, but as Luke 18:19 says, "'Why do you call me good?' Jesus answered. 'No one is good—except God alone.'" (NIV). However, none of us can earn our way into heaven. As Ephesians 2:8-9 says, "For it's by grace you have been saved, through faith—and this is not from yourselves, it's the gift of God—not by works so that no one can boast." (NIV)

Not to say we shouldn't make an effort to be good. The willful sinfulness at the other extreme diminishes our earthly rewards—ranging from grieving God to resulting in negative, even disastrous natural consequences. John Bevere's *Killing Kryptonite* thoroughly explores the effects of willful sinfulness. (Bevere, 2017)

Success is often earned through trial and error—sometimes succeeding and sometimes learning instead. Being deserving of success comes not through piety but through demonstrable value.

Having uncompromising character and integrity in business means those who buy from you receive the value they expect, and those who you work with are respected, valued, and properly compensated. Independent of any spiritual implications, having integrity in business is good for business.

CHOOSING TO BE "THE BOSS"

The modern corporate compensation structure makes achieving a leadership position highly desirable. However, seeking such a position requires great responsibility and a special kind of humility. Too often, we focus on the rewards and benefits rather than the responsibilities and burdens.

It seems that many want to post to social media acting, "like a boss", but they are not willing to make the sacrifices required to really become the boss.

A great leader has the ability to humbly assimilate feedback from their leaders, coaches, customers, and team members in a way that improves performance, rather than leaving them flapping in the breeze and being driven whichever way the wind is blowing.

Managing our enemy, ego, means we are able to receive the kernel of truth in feedback, while discarding the chaff and pain of the delivery. Billionaire hedge fund manager Ray Dalio likes to ask himself, "how do I know I am right?" Taking his ego out of the equation. (Dalio, 2017)

The Christian should be doubly wary of desiring to be a leader because, as James 3:1 says, "Not many of you should become teachers, my fellow believers, because you know that we who teach will be judged more strictly." (NIV)

As leaders, the effects of our actions are multiplied. As we guide our team or organization in a certain direction, our followers move with us—for better or for worse. While each individual is responsible for ensuring they allow the right influences into their lives, the responsibility of the leader is multiplied by the number of people they seek to influence.

BEING VALUABLE

The secret to being deserving of greater rewards is to be of greater value. And the secret to being more valuable is to have capabilities which are rare and in demand. As Cal Newport describes in *So Good They Can't Ignore You*, it's the unique combination of rare *and* valuable that garners greater material rewards. (Newport, 2012)

Corporate strategies often rely on erecting or bene-fiting from barriers to entry in order to make their positions more valuable. The more barriers to legally selling a product, the more defense the company has from others taking their place. For example, a company selling to the healthcare or aviation indus-tries has significant work required to receive regula-tory approval, which prevents most new entrants to the industry.

In the case of the taxi industry, the cab companies and cities conspired to create artificial barriers to entry, which elevated prices. When Uber and Lyft created ride-sharing applications, they skirted (or broke) the existing laws and regulations to revolutionize the industry—supplanting incumbents and decreasing prices for consumers.

People who overcome the barrier to entry for in-demand professions like doctor, lawyer, or engineer, are able to receive more income for the service that they provide, than those who overcome either lower barriers or enter professions which are less in demand.

Motivation expert Earl Nightingale's formula for success was straightforward, "the amount of money we receive will always be in direct ratio to the demand for what we do, our ability to do it, and the difficulty of replacing us." (Nightingale, 1966) In any situation, it's important to be mindful of what we cannot control and to take actions on what we can control. In the case of compensation, it is nearly impossible for an individual to affect supply and demand, but increasing our ability in an area where it is hard to replace us is largely in our control. Nightingale's formula explains why fast food workers are paid so little—there is minimal training required—and why neurosurgeons are highly compensated—it take years and mountains of money to become competent.

In professions that produce celebrities, the supply of contenders is incredibly high, with limited opportunities to make it really, really big. Many, like Adam Corrola, spent years honing their skills in obscurity for little to no money, for the skill that would one day make them famous. (Corolla, 2012) Ultimately, it's only those who do make it, and then write a book about the process from whom we can learn.

For those who do make it, their ability to draw a crowd sets their value, taking us to the extremes of Nightingale's formula. For example, when Donald Trump was an up-and-coming real estate developer with a flair for receiving media attention, The Learning Annex founder Bill Zanker hired the Donald at a yuuuge price, because of the incredible sales and income produced as a result of promoting an event with him—returning much more than was originally invested. (Trump & Zanker, 2008)

The value of drawing crowds and endorsement customers explains why movie stars and major-league sportsballers are paid so much. It's not that they provide immense value to society, it's because they provide immense value to those who hire them.

While it's fine to aspire to reach the upper echelons of success or even celebrity, the daily refinement to become better at what you already do is foundational for future success. Preparing for growth into the next position is only enabled when the primary responsibilities are fulfilled.

For those of the Judeo-Christian heritage, the value of becoming skilled in a trade is highlighted, when in Exodus 35:10, the call goes out for skilled craftsmen in the first step of building the tabernacle, after leaving Egypt for the promised land. These were people who had become skilled with gold, silver, and tent-making before the call from God. They were NOT supernaturally imbued with their capabilities.

CHAPTER FOURTEEN

EARNING YOUR REST

Before you begin to think this chapter will encourage a life of leisure, know the intent instead—to encourage the habit of resting enough to fuel all of the work required to achieving the calling in front of you.

EARNING *THEN* RESTING

Unfortunately, our modern lexicon diminishes the responsibility each of us has in achieving our full potential. We like to say someone is "gifted" or they were born with some "talent." However, whatever seed of ability which resided in someone had to be watered with their blood, sweat, and tears; fertilized with the excrement life gave them; and given the right environment in which to grow.

Overrating the effects of innate talents and gifts accompanied by social media posts of celebrities living the extravagant lifestyle provides the illusion that success comes easily, and the result is unending leisure.

Many are also obsessed with their busyness and hard work, and most of this book is a call to action, which is why there must also be a chapter about resting.

> *Prioritizing rest and good health gives our bodies what they need to make all of the hard work possible.*
> —**Paul Huber** *Killing Complacency*

If you have firmly determined your trajectory, identified how to provide value, and determined to work with definiteness of purpose, you may be driven to work unceasingly toward the success you want. If you only read about rising and grinding and the hard work required for success, without building on a foundation of a rested, healthy body and mind, your inclination might be to not build into your life the rest and recovery needed, to achieve the greatness within you.

Modern science proves the wisdom of Exodus 20:8 when God commanded believers to work six days and rest on the seventh. Changing focus and recuperating after a week of diligent work prepares body and mind for the following week.

> *The sleep of the laborer is sweet...*
> —*Ecclesiastes 5:12 (NIV)*

While the sleep of the laborer is sweet, the sleep of the slacker leads to poverty and despair—just read

Proverbs to see the nearly unending warnings against sloth and excessive rest. Just as sure as planting acorns leads to oak trees, planting a life of little work leads to poverty.

THE RIGHT WAY TO REST

Peak Performance describes the process of first stressing yourself and then recovering through "The Paradox of Rest." In athletic endeavors, your body will tell you when to rest and recover, as the torn muscle fibers and lactic acid provide the stimulus of pain. (Stulberg & Magness, 2017)

Top athletes have mastered the cycle of pain and recovery. As Arnold Schwarzenegger trained for the title of Mr. Universe, his daily workouts included two long muscle-building sessions – one early in the day and one late in the day. Between the sessions, while his muscles were recovering, he built his brain with education and performed the labor needed to fund both the necessities of life, and the growth he needed for his mind and body.

In basketball, training is both mental and physical. Players work to be able to respond intuitively to opponents rather than thinking about their moves. And, a basketballer needs to have the physique to dominate opponents through strength, size, and speed.

In 2018, after having been retired for years, Michael Jordan still made more from endorsements than any active player. When practicing to be the greatest, Jordan allowed his mind and body to recover from the intense workouts by golfing between sessions. This approach allowed his muscles to recover and his brain to register the training at a nearly instinctual level.

The brain uses sleep to connect new facts and motor skills to the existing ones. Not all sleep is equal in this regard, though. The rapid eye movement (REM) sleep associated with dreaming is the most critical sleep to the process, and tends to come after cycles of shallower sleep. Therefore, consistently getting less sleep than you really need is not just causing tiredness; it's also robbing you of the cumulative benefits of learning and building on what you previously learned.

In my own life, I have worked to keep the razor-thin margin between getting enough sleep to keep my mind sharp and to be tired when bedtime rolls around in the evening. Through the routine of getting up at about the same time every day, and then winding down properly and going to bed at about the same time, I have felt the power of the routine to improve my days and nights.

TAMING THE MIND FOR REST

Perhaps one of the biggest disrupters of sleep is worry. We toss and turn, imagining what tomorrow might bring. Biologically, as we attempt to sleep, the rational decision-making part of our brain (the prefrontal cortex) disengages, while the irrational and emotional parts of our brains are continuing to operate…which is why fears in the night seem so much more real than when they are inspected in the morning. (Peters, 2013)

I am not much of a worrier, so just recognizing the roots of nighttime worry was enough to help me sleep easier. Additional strategies for snuffing out night time worry include having a note pad by the bed to write down the concern to be addressed in the morning, and regularly planning actions to control what can be controlled while leaving the rest up to God, fate, chance, or the Universe—depending on what you believe. I choose to control and influence *everything* in my reach while leaving the rest up to God.

ACTIVE RECOVERY

Sleep is not the only form of mental recovery though. Just as athletes use "active recovery" to flush the pain-causing lactic acid from their muscles, active leisure supports active mental recovery.

While we may focus our minds on solving a mathematical problem or writing a paragraph, reducing the focus level does not reduce brain activity. Instead, something called the default-mode network takes over. This powerful network is what provides the answer you had given up on finding through conscious effort. Activities like walking provide sufficient effort to disengage part of the conscious mind and engage the default-mode network.

Perhaps the best analogy I have heard for learning is the growth of coral. Every new thing learned is attached to some pre-existing bit of knowledge. This is part of why the initial phases of education take so long for children – there is no foundation upon which to build. This is also why moving into an adjacent field is much easier than moving into something completely different from your existing experience. It even explains why pneumonic devices and other techniques help us to learn new information easier than we otherwise would.

> *A well-earned night's sleep is far sweeter than an unearned lifestyle of leisure.*
> —**Paul Huber** *Killing Complacency*

CHAPTER FIFTEEN

THE ROAD TO MASTERY

Every journey begins with the first step, but as Yogi Berra said, "If you don't know where you are going, then you'll end up somewhere else." Just as it makes no sense to depart on a road trip with no destination in mind, it makes no sense to go through life without a destination in mind.

> *In life, as in any road trip, there may be detours and time spent discovering unexpected opportunities, but without having an end in mind—definiteness of purpose—the journey will not take you as far as you could have gone.*
> —**Paul Huber** *Killing Complacency*

THE DESTINATION

Returning to the idea that *Talent is Overrated*, the road to mastery can be navigated by anyone willing to put in the work, take the risks, and endure the grind. Our physical and mental abilities are substantial contributors to where we fit best—just as a horse jockey and an NBA star are at opposite ends of the size spectrum, not everyone has the mental capacity to be a doctor or lawyer. However, everyone has the opportunity to be the best in their field.

Those who study emotional intelligence have found intelligence quotient (IQ) influences what field a person enters, but the emotional intelligence quotient (EQ) is an important factor in determining success in the chosen field. And the best news is EQ is far more malleable than IQ. Furthermore, just because someone is not in a celebrated field, should not mean they cannot be celebrated within their field. (Bradberry, 2009)

> *Ultimately, excellence in a person's chosen field, whether world-class or not, is the desired result. If we make excellence in our field our destination, then the process is simple, but not easy.*
> —**Paul Huber** *Killing Complacency*

Producing real and substantial value in any field should always return a commensurate income—if it doesn't you are either overestimating the value of what you do, or failing to negotiate appropriate compensation from your boss or customer.

John Travolta was once surprised by his own value. He wanted to put the Qantas Airlines logo on his Boeing 707 and asked them how much it would cost to use the logo. To his surprise, Qantas wanted to *pay him* to use it. In exchange for Travolta promoting the airline, they paid for the paint job, jet fuel and much more. Both won big—the value of the promotion Qantas received was worth far more than the millions they paid Travolta, who in turn received income for what had once been the very expensive hobby of piloting, maintaining, and fueling his own commercial size jet.

As an aviation enthusiast, Travolta has repeated this feat by gaining sponsorships from regional jet manufacturer Bombardier, and then jumbo jet manufacturer Boeing.

Before he could afford his first jet, Travolta chose to work with a definiteness of purpose—postponing and eventually cutting short his formal education to pursue acting. While he promised his parents he would complete school if acting didn't work out, he pushed hard to make it work so further formal education was unnecessary.

John Travolta has applied to his personal and professional life the same advice he gives to his office staff; there is no need or place for frenzied activity—instead knock down one thing after another so eventually you can become an unstoppable juggernaut.

THE STARTING POINT

Beyond IQ or EQ is deliberate practice. As Anders Ericson discovered in the research presented in *Peak*, IQ appears to be correlated with how quickly a person starts the learning process for a new skill, but it's not correlated with how far they can go with developing the skill. From becoming a chess grandmaster to a memorization savant, the root of these abilities is continually increasing the level of the challenge to build skills. (Erickson & Pool, 2006)

Just as a weight lifter is continually challenging the maximum weight they can lift in order to build the muscle required to lift even more, continually increasing intellectual challenges are required to build the skills residing in the mind.

Just as nobody looks at a weight lifter and says they were born that way, we should not look at a skilled speaker or leader and assume that is just how they were created. It's not through some innate gift they have, and others don't. Instead, they were made that way through their deliberate choices, or in response to the encouragement poured into them by others.

If anything, the gifts given to the "gifted" are encouragement, time and coaching to engage in deliberate practice to build their "gifting." Many sports and musical fields are well studied by pedagogues, who decompose the requisite skills into components well suited to deliberate practice. This is great for those who reach the lucrative pinnacle of the associated entertainment industries. However, we have not given the same attention to building achievement in academic and leadership skills. Not to say sports and arts are not providing value, but instead we could provide much more value in the academic skills needed to build more successful businesses.

They say the best time to plant a tree was 20 years ago and the second-best is today. Your starting point is where you are today—regardless of the deliberate practice you did or did not invest in the past. The destination you choose for yourself may be easier or harder, depending on how you have previously invested in yourself.

Certainly, some athletic competitions, like basketball or football, are so competitive that contenders must start training at an early age to advance before peak physical performance escapes them. However, most pursuits are constrained only by your willingness to commit the needed time and energy to them.

FROM DISASTER TO MASTER

The path from disaster to master of any skill is straightforward—but not easy. Chapter 10 introduced the process of *The First 20 Hours* of deliberate practice facilitating a foundational level of skill, and subsequent thousands of hours to become world-class in the most competitive fields. Those who have become masters report the required deliberate practice is not fun or easy—but it's worth it to achieve or maintain their status as among the best at what they do.

By following your purposeful ambition, it's possible to deliberately choose which skills to improve. In some cases, you may choose to pull up an anchor holding you in place, or you may choose to build in an area where you are very good—making a more powerful engine to propel yourself in the sea of life. The deliberate practice required to get better won't be fun or easy, but it will be worth the investment to fulfill your purposeful ambitions. Navigating the motivation dip between initial competence and greatness is made easier when you have a powerful why driving you—something giving purpose to your ambition.

DELIBERATE PRACTICE

Applying deliberate practice is much more than spending hours grinding away at an activity. Instead, putting the *deliberate* in deliberate practice requires prompt feedback, and incrementally more challenging skills to practice. It's the piano teacher moving the student from *Old MacDonald's Farm* to Beethoven's piano sonatas through incrementally more challenging pieces. It's the golf pro who records your swing and tells you how to correct it… and then hitting a bucket of balls with your improved technique, while watching how each ball responds to your swing.

Sports provide endless metaphors for life and business; beyond the metaphors, though, sports and music provide objective and immediate feedback unavailable elsewhere. Business leaders make informed decisions about improving their businesses, but the feedback often doesn't arrive until the end of the quarter or even years later. This is what makes mastering business leadership so challenging.

Anyone seeking to improve an area without immediate feedback should find ways to shorten the feedback cycle, or break down the skill into more discrete and quantifiable subskills. Process frameworks like scrum and agile which originated in the software development realm, measure the results of development sprints in time boxes ranging from one week to one month, rather than requiring a development cycle of a year or longer. This shorter development timeline allows for feedback and course correction after each sprint rather than at the very end of a multi-year project.

SKILL STACKING

Because there is no limit to how far deliberate practice can take a person in their chosen skill, someone with purposeful ambition will choose which set of skills to focus on building and maintaining. The rest will not be pursued or allowed to atrophy through disuse. This is the art of focusing on *The One Thing* driving your ambition to the exclusion of all else. (Keller & Papasan, 2013)

Wisely stacking one skill on top of another in support of your purposeful ambition maximizes the benefit from the investments you are making in deliberate practice.

Choosing the right set of skills to consistently work on compounds into succeeding in the area of your purposeful ambition.

SHUHARI

Japanese martial arts represent the road to mastery through the concept of shuhari. Each syllable in the English transliteration represents one of the three levels of growth within the discipline.

> **Shu**, the beginning stage, is simple obedience. The sensei who has mastered the art is teaching fundamental moves and wisdom distilled into proverbs.

> **Ha**, literally branching, is when the student moves away from the rote basics and learns the theory and underlying principles of the art.

> **Ri** is the transcendence of the art. At this point, the master understands the art so well they are able to be innovative.

The wisdom in this approach is that the oft-maligned rote memorization is actually the foundational antecedent to a productive understanding, which precedes the mastery needed for innovation.

When I attempt to take artistic license before reaching the Ri stage, my friends will rightly tell me that my license should be revoked (or was never actually issued). Without a transcendent understanding of a topic, it's unreasonable to expect to be able to push it into the adjacent possible.

FLOW

Perhaps the optimal state of mind is the state of flow, as coined by Mihaly Csikszentmihalyi. During the flow state, the mental challenge is high enough to demand full attention with some stretching, but not great enough to cause panic or distress. During flow, all sense of time and the world beyond slips away as the full focus of the mind is channeled at a single task. (Csikszentmihalyi, 1997)

Flow is the opposite of multitasking. While multi-tasking provides the illusion of increased product-ivity by accomplishing multiple tasks at once, the reality is that the brain is rapidly switching between multiple sequential tasks—and performing all of them sub-optimally.

The better approach is to provide sequential focus to each task, achieving flow during the most important tasks—the ones you are uniquely qualified to perform.

HABIT STACKING

Just as skill stacking is deliberately selecting the skills aligning with your purposeful ambition, habit stacking allows you to purposefully select habits which lead to your goals. Perhaps part of your morning routine, like mine, is a series of hygiene habits—shaving, brushing teeth, showering, dressing, deodorizing, and applying hair product. This means the best looking and smelling version of you is out in public.

Stacking more positive habits into your day means accomplishing the other important tasks in your life becomes nearly automatic. Most importantly, stacking one small but important habit on another does not require you to make one giant leap, but instead a series of small steps.

S.J. Scott's definition of *Habit Stacking* is:

1. Identify those small important actions (like writing a loving message to the important people in your life).

2. Group them together into a routine with equally important actions.

3. Schedule a specific time each day to complete this routine.

4. Use a trigger as a reminder to complete this stack.

5. Make it super easy to get started. (Scott, 2017)

PURPOSEFUL EXPLORATION

While focusing on the skills and habits needed for fulfilling your purposeful ambition is important, the purposeful exploration of ideas in unrelated areas presents an opportunity to improve your life, your contribution to your business, and maybe even giving you the opportunity to become very rich.

Purposeful exploration provides your brain with the novelty it seeks and the opportunity to learn something unexpected. The next time you come across a news-stand, or are channel surfing past some documentaries, consider landing on something you would not otherwise choose. In addition to expanding your knowledge, this approach gives you an opportunity to intelligently discuss a topic with a new acquaintance—at least enough to ask intelligent questions about their area of expertise.

What do these five business concepts have in common:

- Distressed inventory

- Soft goods fulfillment

- Perishable commodities

- Online consumers

- Dynamic pricing

The answer, not so obviously, is www.**priceline.com**.

When Jeff Hoffman was reviewing these concepts with Jay Walker, all of the pieces eventually fell into place:

- The airlines dynamically update prices based on the available "inventory" of seats on upcoming flights.

- Ideally (for the airline), the seats are sold at the absolute highest price. However, if a seat would otherwise go unsold, just about any reasonable price is enough to boost the profitability of that particular flight.

- Seats are perishable commodities–as soon as the flight takes off, only the seats that have been sold provide value to the airline.

> *Priceline provides value to the consumers by giving them the lowest price available and provides value to the airlines by selling as many seats as possible.*
> —**Paul Huber** *Killing Complacency*

Jeff Hoffman performs what he calls "Info Sponging;" a disciplined approach to developing breadth. The breadth of ideas, trends, and concepts—purposefully creating a breeding ground for new ideas.

The process is simple, and should be done as frequently as possible—every day if you can:

- Spend 20 minutes info sponging—no disruptions.

- Mentally leave your industry, your business, your domain, your discipline.

    o Review cross-disciplinary content:
    e.g., banking, pharmaceuticals, restaurants, entertainment, search the top ten trends etc.

- Take notes of what piques your curiosity– everything interesting to you.

- Review the list of data points at the end of the session.

Eventually, after enough sessions, a picture forms–assembling the pieces of the puzzle. The result is your next opportunity to provide value to the world.

SPECIAL BONUS OFFER
GO TO
pauljhuber.com/kc-bonuses
to download exclusive
content for readers of
Killing Complacency.

CHAPTER SIXTEEN

FROM COMPLACENCY TO GROWTH

The battle against complacency lasts a lifetime. I hope, for an increasing number of people, complacency loses and positive success wins. Sure, it won't be all of the time, but the trend can shift—if you make the effort to push it. Our nature favors rest, comfort, and ultimately complacency. Only through the recognition of complacency can we begin to battle it.

COMPLACENCY FIGHTS A TOUGH BATTLE

Our nature is to envy when instead, we should use the success of others for motivation. Our nature is to feel guilty for having success when instead; we should give to what inspires us so others are inspired too. Our nature is to seek comfort when instead; we should be comfortable being uncomfortable in order to grow. Our nature is to sedate the pains in life when instead; we should face the pain in order to heal.

> *Our nature is to become complacent.*

Healthy ambitions help us to overcome complacency with drive. Properly applying our drive allows us to focus on the success required of us without neglecting our health and our family.

SUCCESS IS YOUR DUTY

Nobody's success is robbing you of the opportunity to create your own success. However, those afflicted with complacency and rejecting success may rob others of their success, as the successful are called upon to support the complacent.

At the 2020 Growth Conference, comedian Kevin Hart and Grant Cardone were discussing the differences in mindset between the rich and the poor. Both had grown up poor and worked their way into success, so they were speaking from experience. Grant's assertion was the poor see everything they don't understand as a scam, where as the rich work to understand opportunities so they can decide whether or not it's a prudent investment.

Kevin's response was the poor see everything as a scam because they *are* being scammed all of the time. Too many of our poor are surrounded by check cashing and liquor stores. Rather than being encouraged to join the mainstream of society with checking and savings accounts, income is immediately converted to cash and then into alcohol and money orders for bills. Rather than spiraling upward to success, the drugs, alcohol, and lifestyle of their community is pulling them downward.

Instead of perpetuating the situation, Kevin is working with JP Morgan Chase to improve financial literacy in inner cities which will help people differentiate between actual scams and opportunities for growth.

Taking responsibility for success means taking responsibility for differentiating between a scam and a legitimate opportunity. Differentiating between the two requires learning about an area of opportunity—though, not necessarily in a classroom. And while it's possible to be successful on many fronts, everyone who has achieved multi-front success was first successful in one area, and then moved into another and another.

As Grant Cardone said, what you need is not sympathy or empathy for your current situation; what you need is help to move to a better situation. Rather than lamenting your position, or a handout, what you need is to accept and apply the help necessary to move up.

Magic Johnson first achieved basketball success and then business success because even when he was poor, he didn't have poor dreams. He is relentless in his pursuit of more success so he can leave a legacy of prosperity rather than poverty. (Also from the 2020 Growth Conference.)

GROWTH IS YOUR RESPONSIBILITY

As the CEO of You Inc., the task of growing is not only your responsibility; it's also one you cannot

delegate. Your personal trainer can't lift weights to build your muscles. You can hire a musician to play for you, but the transaction won't give you the ability to play your favorite song.

> *If you want success, you must have the skills needed to produce value.*
> *If you want the skills, you must do the work.*
> —**Paul Huber** *Killing Complacency*

While a person's first priority is to build skills that contribute to their financial wellbeing, becoming skilled at relationships and hobbies is also important for increasing satisfaction in life.

As CEO, it's your responsibility first to develop a strategy to improve your results in each important area of life, and then to execute it.

COACHING FOR SUCCESS

In the quest to build the self-esteem and self-worth of believers, preachers and parents like to say, "God doesn't make junk." While it's certainly true God values every human, the sentiment that He doesn't make junk, combined with the fixed mindset metastasizes into denying problems or failing to seize opportunities for growth. Bumper stickers usually don't make for good doctrine. The more helpful truth for the believer is that you are God's work in process—He will mold you through your experiences and through the influence of those around you.

> *God values you, AND He expects you to put in a lot of work during the growth process.*
> —**Paul Huber** *Killing Complacency*

Perhaps the most amazing ability God gave humans is our ability to adapt and grow. This amazing ability comes with the frustrating factor that growth only comes through effort, which is often accompanied by physical or mental pain—just ask anyone who has worked out or had to learn math. We are hard-wired to avoid pain or at least delay it—the pain of potential health problems in the distant future seems inconsequential, compared to the near-term pain of exercising or foregoing dessert. However, the rewards of fitness and math skills outweigh the shorter-term pain.

As imperfect people in this imperfect world, it's OK to admit you are not OK. But it's not OK to not do something about it—to do your part as God does His. It's OK to have a broken foot, but it's not OK to avoid having it treated by a doctor so it can heal properly. It's OK to feel down, but it's not OK to not reach out to

friends and family for comfort. It's OK to be depressed, but it's not OK to not get professional help. It's OK to have a permanent disability, but it's not OK to avoid taking the right steps to compensate for it. OK?

Just as we need to address what is not OK with ourselves, we also have a responsibility to make the most of what we have. Just as we have professionals who can take care of what is broken, there are professionals who can make us the best versions of ourselves. Fitness coaches can help train our bodies and success coaches, or life coaches can help train our minds. The frustration factor, though, is you cannot outsource the work to your coaches. YOU have to lift the weights and run the miles. YOU have to do the homework and execute your plans. All a coach can do is give you the exercises and review your technique—the rest is up to you.

THOUGHTS ARE [NO]THINGS

How we respond and react to our thoughts is critical. However, being critical of our thoughts can cause new problems. While the Apostle Paul liked to take thoughts captive (1 Corinthians 10:5), wrestling ones that we don't like into a jail cell simply amplifies the negative impacts of those thoughts.

The better approach is to see our thoughts as clouds in the sky, or cars on the road. (Puddicimbe, 2012) They are something that exists, but we can objectively view them and evaluate if the thought is something that aligns with our values, and is something we want to pursue. If a thought passes that you don't like or doesn't align with what you want to be, visualize it walking by into an inaccessible jail cell, rather than attempting to subdue and arrest it—giving it time to attach you. Alternatively, view it as a car on the road passing by, or a leaf on a stream that comes into view and then leaves.

As the owners of our minds, we have the ability—the responsibility—to act as traffic director. We have the responsibility to choose who we want to be, and then direct the thoughts that drive us to the actions that will lead us to our desired results.

> *A passing thought is nothing.*
> *A thought pursued becomes*
> *something.*
> —**Paul Huber** *Killing Complacency*

Thoughts are things, as successful mindset expert Bob Proctor says. Everything that exists started as a thought. If you believe that God created the universe, He thought about it before He created it. Everything that we build on this earth that He created, someone thinks of it before it is built.

Whether it results from your environment, your decisions, or divine intervention, the initial existence

of an individual thought is nothing more than an electrical impulse in your brain. The more time that you spend pushing traffic through a certain part of your brain, the more it strengthens its ability to handle that traffic. Therefore, a passing thought is nothing to worry about—instead direct your energy toward choosing where you want most of your thoughts to head; spend time creating the person who you want to be.

GROWING INTO YOUR NEXT OPPORTUNITY

While some fail to act due to a lack of confidence, other's irrational confidence produces acts of failure. To confront manufactured confidence, John Maxwell advises to focus on growth on the inside, rather than growth on the [false] outside. (Maxwell J. , 2019)

To grow real confidence, first consider how to produce a small win where you need confidence. Then find an opportunity to tackle a larger version. Scientific analysis discovered that a domino can topple another domino one and a half times bigger than itself. Progressively growing capability by fifty percent will quickly result in the ability to achieve massive goals. Most importantly, learning from mistakes while accomplishing the smaller goals will prepare you for the ability to overcome the massive goal, that you only hoped that would "one day" be accomplished.

Once a level of proficiency has been achieved, consider how to multiply the results by ten. The crux of the 10X rule is simply doubling effort to double results eventually becomes impossible with finite time and energy. Instead, a new paradigm is required to achieve increased results. (Cardone, 2011)

The 10X lifestyle absolutely requires massive action; but it also requires the willingness to overcome paradigms that don't work and openness to coaching.

True humility is not self-loathing, but a willingness to consider input from your results, your friends, and even your haters… and sorting the useful data from the useless.

LIVING OUT THE GROWTH MINDSET

Living out the growth mindset is not easy—but it's rewarding in this abundant world:

- **Challenges** are not there to provide misery but to provide opportunities to grow—choose to confront them the way David did with the lions and the bears.
- **Obstacles** are not there to stop you but to deter those who would challenge you. Overcoming an obstacle provides the path to your success.
- **Effort** is not some evil plan to torment you, but it's the divine order for life on this earth.
- **Criticism** may be sent your way to hurt you, but any nugget of truth is beneficial for your growth.
- **Other's success** should not spark envy but provide inspiration for your success. There is enough water in the ocean to float everyone's boat.

SPECIAL BONUS OFFER
GO TO
pauljhuber.com/kc-bonuses
to download exclusive
content for readers of
Killing Complacency.

CHAPTER SEVENTEEN

YOUR PLAN

SET YOUR TRAJECTORY

A pilot navigating from New York to Los Angeles does a lot more than take off and aim at the destination. At lower altitudes, variable winds push the plane in one direction and then another—requiring constant adjustments to the trajectory of the plane. At higher altitudes, the jet stream constantly slows the progress of the plane and pushes it off course. Due to the effects of the jet stream, a plane flying at an airspeed of 600 miles per hour may only cover 500 miles of ground in an hour, due to the air moving opposite to the desired direction.

Though we may experience headwinds and being bounced off course, choosing a trajectory of success will head us toward success. Knowing the destination will allow us to make course corrections. Rerouting to a new destination is far easier if you are on track to somewhere, rather than heading nowhere.

MEASURE YOUR ACTIONS

Actions precede results—often by a long time. Sustaining the drive to results is far easier if, instead

of just measuring results, you also measure the actions required to get the results. When I lost 35 pounds on a diet, they were not gone the instant I decided I wanted to get rid of them. This book didn't write itself the moment I decided a one-page study on "The Growth Mindset and an Infinite God" deserved a lot more than just ten pages.

Instead, the pounds were lost as each meal and snack accumulated into less than the calories I needed for the day—forcing my body to burn fat. Tracking everything I consumed showed me immediately that my actions were aligned with reducing my weight—regardless of daily fluctuations in my weight. Eventually, the diet had the desired result—even if I could not see, feel, or intuit the results from a single meal.

Actions to complete this book were measured in hours in my home office or in local coffee shops. Eventually, all of the words added to pages and pages to chapters, but it took a lot of actions for outlining, editing, and reading about writing to get to the finished product.

MEASURE YOUR RESULTS

Eventually, actions accumulate into results. Eventually, the pounds melt away, the waistline recedes, and a healthy you emerges. Just like the consistent blogger or social media marketer eventually sees their audience explode, to the point where their side hustle becomes their day job.

Eventually, your accumulated actions will take you somewhere. However, it may be much slower than you would like—so be prepared by learning about how long it takes others who have achieved a similar goal.

ADJUST YOUR PLAN

In addition to your plans being thwarted by external forces, sometimes your plans are not the right ones for your desired results. Perhaps you read all of the right books, learned from all the wise counsel you could find, and still, the desired results are not following the sustained actions.

At this point, analyzing your plan and the actions taken can help pinpoint the required adjustments. During my time in process improvement, we had a mantra of "plan, do, check, adjust." If the actions are not producing the desired results, it's time to analyze and adjust.

In the case of Bravo TV reality star Ryan Serhant, the planned goal was to become successful—and his adjustment went as far as changing from desiring success in acting to pursuing success in real estate. By leveraging the skills he learned attempting to become an actor, he was able to better play to the camera in a reality TV show—further boosting his real estate success. (Serhant, 2019)

Grit, of one form or another is required to achieve success—whether driving Plan A to a successful conclusion, or continually pivoting until Plan T finally achieves success. Successfully discerning between the time to pivot and the time to stay the course is a crucial determinant of achieving success, rather than endlessly working for a goal that will never arrive.

SUCCEED

Your mission, your obligation, and your duty in this life is to succeed—in all of your roles. The world offers nearly limitless abundance—your role is to help others obtain their portion as you obtain yours. Every successful honest business is there to help people in some way—and the more we help one another, the more our businesses grow.

You may lead your own business or feel like just another cog in someone else's business. Either way, your success and the success of your labor is needed in this world.

SPECIAL BONUS OFFER
GO TO
pauljhuber.com/kc-bonuses
to download exclusive
content for readers of
Killing Complacency.

NOTES AND BIBLIOGRAPHY

BIBLIOGRAPHY

Acuff, J. (2011). *Quitter: Closing the Gap Between Your Day Job and Your Dream Job.* Brentwood, TN: Lampo Press.

Batterson, M. (2016). *Chase the Lion: If Your Dream Doesn't Scare You, It's Too Small.* Colorado Springs, CO: Multnomah.

Bevere, J. (2017). Called. Messenger International.

Bevere, J. (2017). *Killing Kryptonite: Destroy What Steals Your Strength.* Messenger International.

Bohannon, L. F. (2019). *Beginner's Pluck: Build Your Life of Purpose and Impact Now.* Baker Books.

Bradberry, T. (2009). *Emotional Intelligence 2.0.* TalentSmart.

Branson, R. (2014). *The Virgin Way: Everything I Know about Leadership.* Portfolio .

Byrne, R. (2006). *The Secret.* Hillsboro, OR: Beyond Words. Cardone, G . (2011). *The 10X Rule: The Only Difference Between Success and Failure.* Wiley.

Cardone, G. (2016). *Be Obsessed or Be Average.* New York: Penguin.

Christensen, C. (1997). *The Innovator's Dilemma: When New Technologies Cause Great Firms to Fail.* Harvard Business Review Press.

Colvin, G. (2008). *Talent Is Overrated: What Really Separates World-Class Performers from Everybody Else.* New York, NY: Penguin Group.

Corolla, A. (2012). *Not Taco Bell Material.* Crown Archetype.

Cox, W. M., & Alm, R. (1995). By Our Own Bootstraps: Economic Opportunity & the Dynamics of Income Distribution. *Annual Report, Federal Reserve Bank of Dallas*, 8.

Csikszentmihalyi, M. (1997). *Finging Flow: The Psychology of Engagement.* New York: BasicBooks.

Dalio, R. (2017). *Principles: Life and Work.* Simon & Schuster.

Dexter, P. (1986). *Deadwood.* New York: Random House.

Duckworth, A. (2016). *Grit: the Power of Passion and Perseverance.* Scribner.

Dweck, C. (2006). *Mindset: The New Psychology of Success.* Ballantine Books.

Eker, T. H. (2009). *Secrets of the Millionaire Mind: Mastering the Inner Game of Wealth.* HarperCollins.

Erickson, K. A., & Pool, R. (2006). *Peak: Secrets from the New Science of Expertise.* Eamon Dolan/Houghton Mifflin Harcourt.

Fertitta, T., & Gray, J. (2019). *Shut Up and Listen!: Hard Business Truths that Will Help You Succeed.* HarperCollins.

For the Least of These. (2014). Grand Rapids, MI: Zondervan.

Foster, J. (2004). *Life Focus.* Grand Rapids, MI: Fleming H. Revell.

Frankl, V. (1959). *Man's Search for Meaning.*

Gladwell, M. (2008). *Outliers: The Story of Success.* Little, Brown and Company.

Gladwell, M. (2009). *What the Dog Saw: And Other Adventures.* Little, Brown and Company.

Godin, S. (2007). *The Dip: A Little Book That Teaches You When to Quit (and When to Stick).* Portfolio.

Goggins, D. (2018). *Can't Hurt Me: Master Your Mind and Defy the Odds.* Lioncrest Publishing.

Haden, J. (2018). *The Motivation Myth.* Portfolio/Penguin.

Hagan, S. (2019). *The Language of Influence and Power.* Minneapolis, MN: KPT Publishing.

Hardy, D. (2010). *The Compound Effect: Multiplying your success, one simple step at a time.* New York: Vanguard Press.

Harvey, D. (2010). *Rescuing Ambition.* Crossway.

Hill, N. (1937). *Think and Grow Rich.* The Ralston Society.

Hill, N. (2012). *Napoleon Hill's Outwitting the Devil: The Secret to Freedom and Success.* Sterling Publishing.

Hoffman, B. (2013). *American Icon: Alan Mulally and the Fight to Save Ford Motor Company.* Currency.

Holiday, R. (2016). *Ego is the Enemy.* New York: Portfolio / Penguin.

Jakes, T. D. (2019). *Crushing: God Turns Pressure into Power.* FaithWords.

John, D. (2016). *The Power of Broke: How Empty Pockets, a Tight Budget, and a Hunger for Success Can Become Your Greatest Competitive Advantage.* Currency.

John, D. (2018). *Rise and Grind: Outperform, Outwork, and Outhustle Your Way to a More Successful and Rewarding Life.* Currency.

Kaufman, J. (2013). *The First 20 Hours: How to Learn Anything... Fast!* Portfolio .

Keller, G., & Papasan, J. (2013). *The ONE Thing: The Surprisingly Simple Truth Behind Extraordinary Results.* Bard Press.

Kim, W. C., & Maubourgne, R. (2014). *Blue Ocean Strategy.* Harvard Business Review Press.

Kiyosaki, R. (2009). *Rich Dad Poor Dad: What The Rich Teach Their Kids About Money -That The Poor And Middle Class Do Not!* Plata Publishing.

Kübler-Ross, E. (1973). *On Death and Dying.* Routledge.

Liker, J. (2004). *The Toyota Way: 14 Management Principles from the World's Greatest Manufacturer.* McGraw-Hill Education.

Martin, S. (2007). *Born Standing Up: A Comic's Life.* Scribner.

Maxwell, J. (2019). *Leadershift: the 11 Essential Changes Every Leader Must Embrace.* HarperCollins Leadership.

Maxwell, J. C. (2015). *Sometimes You Win--Sometimes You Learn: Life's Greatest Lessons Are Gained from Our Losses .* Center Street.

Newport, C. (2012). *So Good They Can't Ignore You: Why Skills Trump Passion in the Quest for Work You Love.* Grand Central Publishing .

Nightingale, E. (1966). *Lead the Field.* Shippensburg, PA: Nightingale Conant Corporation.

Peters, S. (2013). *The Chimp Paradox: The Mind Management Program to Help You Achieve Success, Confidence, and Happiness.* TarcherPerigee.

Pira, A. (2019). *Homeless to Billionaire: the 18 Principles for Wealth Attraction and Creating Unlimited Opportunities.* Charleston, SC: ForbesBooks.

Ponder, C. (1962). *How to Live a Prosperous Life.* Martino Fine Books.

Pressfield, S. (2002). *The War of Art: Break Through the Blocks and Win Your Inner Creative Battles.* New York: Black Irish Entertainment LLC.

Pressfield, S. (2012). *Turning Pro: Tap Your Inner Power and Create Your Life's Work.* Black Irish Books.

Pressfiled, S. (2016). *Nobody Wants to Red Your Sh*t: Why That is and What You Can Do About It.* Black Irish Entertainment.

Puddicimbe, A. (2012). *The Headspace Guide to Meditation and Mindfulness: How Mindfulness Can Change Your Life in Ten Minutes a Day* . St. Martin's Griffin.

Rogers, D. E. (2003). *Diffusion of Innovations.* Free Press.

Schiff, P. D., & Schiff, A. J. (2010). *How An Economy Grows And Why It Crashes.* Wiley.

Schwarzenegger, A. (2012). *Total Recall: My Unbelievably True Life Story.* Simon & Schuster.

Scott, S. (2017). *Habit Stacking: 127 Small Changes to Improve Your Health, Wealth, and Happiness.* Oldtown Publishing LLC.

Serhant, R. (2019). *Sell it Like Serhant: How to Sell More, Earn More, and Become the Ultimate Sales Machine.* New York: Hachette Books.

Sowell, T. (2005). *Black Rednecks and White Liberals.* Encounter Books.

Sowell, T. (2016). *Wealth, Poverty and Politics.* Basic Books.

Stulberg, B., & Magness, S. (2017). *Peak Performance: Elevate Your Game, Avoid Burnout, and Thrive with the New Science of Success.* Rodale Books.

Townsend, D. J. (2015). *The Entitlement Cure: Finding Success in Doing Hard Things the Righ Way.* Grand Rapids, MI: Zondervan.

Trump, D., & Zanker, B. (2008). *Think Big: Make it Happen in Business and Life.* HarperBusiness.

Welch, J. (2009). *Winning: The Ultimate Business How-To Book.* Harper Collins.

Whelchel, H. (2012). *How Then Should We Work.* McLean, VA: Institute for Faith, Work & Economics.

White, G. J. (2017). *WarriorBook: How to Master the Art and Science of Having it All.* Austin, Tx: Next Century Publishing.

SPECIAL BONUS OFFER
GO TO
pauljhuber.com/kc-bonuses
to download exclusive
content for readers of
Killing Complacency.

ONE LAST THING AND THANKS

If you enjoyed this book or found it useful, I would be very grateful if you would post a short review on Amazon. Your support really does make a difference, and I read all the reviews personally so I can get your feedback and make this book and future books even better.

THANKS!

This book was published thanks to free support and training from:

www.EbookPublishingSchool.com
www.StoryGrid.com

Shawn Coyne's *Story Grid* book was immensely helpful in organizing the thoughts in this book—and hopefully making it an interesting journey for the reader. Shawn's business partner, Steven Pressfield, provided both useful insights about writing in *Nobody Wants to Read Your Sh*t*, and motivation in *The War of Art* and *Turning Pro*. (Pressfiled, 2016) (Pressfield, 2002) (Pressfield, 2012)

Carolyn Flower and her team at Oxygen Publishing were instrumental in pulling the book over the finish line—including designing the cover and helping me through the editing and independent publishing process.

ABOUT THE AUTHOR

PAUL HUBER

Trained as a computer engineer, Paul has spent over twenty years at a leading aerospace and defense company developing safety-critical, embedded computer systems. The technical challenges of engineering have been smaller than dealing with the people challenges. The opposing mindsets of perfectionism and complacency have often been the greatest challenges. Paul has a Bachelor's of Science in Computer Engineering from the South Dakota School of Mines and Technology, a Master's of Systems Engineering from Iowa State University, and a Master's of Business Administration from the Jack Welch Management Institute at Strayer University. *Killing Complacency* represents Paul's doctoral dissertation for the Drivetime University School of Motivation.

Learn more about Paul's books at **www.amazon.com**

Learn more about Paul at **www.PaulJHuber.com**

Made in the USA
Monee, IL
11 July 2020